BEYOND SURVIVAL:
Thriving in Your First Years of Teaching

Cheryl Barnard

Published by Deep Roots Publishing
Calgary, Alberta ©2010

Deep Roots Publishing
Calgary, Alberta
1-866-309-3622

Front and back covers designed by Stuart Barnard

Printed in Calgary, Alberta
Blitzprint Inc
Suite 1, 1235 64th Avenue, SE
Calgary, Alberta Canada T2H 2J7

ISBN 10 – 1-453-84097-4
ISBN 13- 978-1-45-384097-9

To Teachers

Acknowledgements

"I am a part of all I have met." - Alfred Lord Tennyson
(1809 ~ 1892)

I truly believe in the lines above and therefore, there a great many people in my life to thank. First and foremost, my parents who modelled hard work and made me feel I could do anything I set my mind to. Thanks for your love, patience, selfless sacrifice and belief in me. Stuart and Jenni, your unbelievable enthusiasm and encouragement have been key. Thanks especially Stu for your web expertise, and Jen, Isaac and Jonah for the joy you bring. Steve, you have always stayed true to yourself and your passion for what you do has rubbed off, thanks!

Terrance and Moira, your unconditional love and encouragement have been solid ground for me whenever things got shaky. Thanks for listening to all the ins and outs, dreams and plans. April, you too have been a safe haven, a tremendous listener and a huge cheerleader. Les, you have always made me believe in possibilities, and since I met you, have always encouraged me to pursue my best. Sonya, thanks for wanting and wishing for my best. Loretta, times with you are never as frequent as I'd like, but your words of wisdom are forever etched on my heart, and encourage me daily. Betty, your goal-setting and accountability were instrumental in getting this down on paper and Heather, your coaching instrumental in helping me believe in my passions and abilities and to dare to dream.

And to the educators; model teachers in my life such as Mrs. Rohovie who challenged me to challenge myself, and Mrs. Renyk who gifted me with a love of the written word and showed me how a true master teacher teaches. Speaking of masters, I must acknowledge Drs. Michael Pollard, Robin Bright and Leah Fowler. Your combined, tag-team classes to Language Arts teachers are among my greatest gems in education.

St. Catherine's School, Picture Butte, a phenomenal staff and especially to Mr. Terry Wilson, thanks for giving me such an amazing practicum experience.

Trinity Christian School – my face lights as I write your name. It's July now and I can't wait to get back to you in the fall. You are like family, and I dearly love the school community. To Stan, you are an amazing leader and the way you empower your staff is incredible. It is a great honour to be a part of your team. To Lynda, thank you for taking the time to closely read this cover to cover. Your opinion, questions and admonitions were so helpful in the process. You are a great mentor and I so value your input in my life, thanks for journeying with me. TCS Staff, I can't list you all – but thank you, thank you, thank you; I am so blessed to live, work and play with you and among you.

Lord, above all I want to thank you. Thank you for the profession of teaching and the incredible calling it is to inspire, educate and instruct. Thank you for this opportunity; may it travel to where it might be of most help and encourage those that need it.

Table of Contents

Preface

Before Digging Deep

1. Your Teaching Self   **15**

Learning to Laugh and Relax the Perfectionist Within

2. Staffroom Climate: From Tension to Teamwork   **27**

Competition, Comparison and Collaboration of Staff

3. Dealing with Co-workers   **39**

Beware of the Moaners, Martyrs and Misfits

4. Classroom Management: **51**

Why Bricks are Better Than Elastics Any Day

5. The Essence of Teaching   **63**

Truly Making an Impact

6. Life / Work Balance in Teaching   **85**

Tire-Pressure Monitoring System

7. Dealing with Parents   **95**

Standing Tall: Even With a Parent's Call

8. Making Learning Meaningful   **109**

To Never Ask Why?

9. Celebrate!   **119**

Marking Milestones with Celebration

Preface

"Good teaching cannot be reduced to technique; good teaching comes from the identity and integrity of the teacher…, it depends less on the methods I use than on the degree to which I know and trust my selfhood – and am willing to make it available and vulnerable in the service of learning. Good teachers share one trait: a strong sense of personal identity infuses their work."

Parker J. Palmer
The Courage to Teach

What makes teaching so all-consuming and coincidently so draining and demanding, is that so often it is an extension of our very selves. So often it is our hearts, our passions, our enthusiasm for life, for learning or for a specific subject area that is daily on the line. Our hearts are forever on our sleeves, sometimes at the mercy of everyone around us. Co-workers may mock our zeal, administration may think it not enough, parents determine it too much or too little and students are either too young or too cool to care.

And so – what shall become of this passion? Good teaching is oh so good because so much of the "self" permeates everything: in each lesson, in each caring comment on an essay, in each literary selection or enthusiastic explanation of a math strategy or scientific experiment. Because the majority of what teachers do is an extension of themselves, the way that others respond can often wield a powerful hold. We are engineered to shy away from pain; we are programmed to change, to adapt. If something so personal is handled with such scorn, disdain or inadequacy, we are programmed to seek protection, to flee the hurt and put up the wall. So is the case with many facets of life. A scorned lover eventually learns to retreat, deny feelings

> *…The majority of what teachers do is an extension of themselves…*

9

and move on. An unsuccessful businessman learns to either change his tactics or change his profession. Where does that leave us in the realm of teaching?

I learned early on that if I continued to look for fulfillment and measure my success by the reactions of my fourteen and fifteen year old students, I was on the fast track to leaving the teaching profession forever. The lessons came hard and fast at first and were somewhat proportionate to the time I had invested in a given task. After creating a game board as a test review and staying up all night laminating and cutting out each piece, I was certain that this game would wipe the typical "come on – just try to impress me" look off my students' faces forever. Not only would they enjoy this review but they would also be able to look back on my class as one of the highlights of their educational careers. Talk about setting myself up for defeat! I had to nudge them

> *If I continued to measure my success by the reactions of my students, I was on the fast track to leaving the profession.*

along just as much as any other day; no one even noticed the laminated pieces, nor did they care that I had made it! I felt like a failure and worse than that, I felt unappreciated.

Such lessons repeated themselves time and time again and in all different contexts. Such foolishness was not limited to my interactions with students alone. I thought for sure parents would appreciate the time and care I put into their son or daughter's report card commentary, or that my administration would take note of my especially detailed year plans, or that my colleague would congratulate me on a particularly excellent lesson – the list could go on and on.

But then it hit me. It hit me like a ton of bricks! It was **I** who was truly causing my feelings of defeat. I was looking to these outside sources for significance and affirmation. I essentially put my career in the hands of others, asking them to legitimize my teaching, to validate my

> *I had put my career in the hands of others.*

suitability and somehow hope that they could dispel my feelings of insecurity as a professional. I placed myself on a roller coaster of success and failure countless times each and every day.

What lies at the heart of this issue is in fact something good, something that is essential to quality teaching - the fact that the self is infused in everything. That is a good thing and usually the mark of a gifted, passionate teacher. The problem arises when questions and doubts about the "self" create a situation in which I allow my profession to dictate how I feel about my "self". It is a delicate balance; listening to outside sources to help refine you as a teacher, but then giving enough weight to your own personal reflections and knowledge of yourself. Because so much of ourselves is exposed in teaching, a rebuff or a failure within the classroom or school community can easily be translated to personal chastisement or defeat. My identity as a teacher and my growth as a professional, are the result of a balanced mixture of personal reflection and feedback from colleagues, administrators, students and parents. In my first few years of teaching, I gave unequal weight in those equations and was heading down a path of dissatisfaction and feelings of failure.

> *It is a delicate balance...*

I had to take back my dream profession. I had to take back possession of my feelings towards my teaching, my planning, my classroom management, everything. I had to believe in my training. I had to believe that I was doing the very best I could each and every day. I had to give myself grace, give myself freedom to make mistakes, and know that each day I was seeking to love my students and encourage in them a love of learning. I also had to give myself a reality check, to remind myself that the career I had chosen wasn't one where moments were prescribed with policies, procedures and protocol, but instead was a dynamic, ever-evolving, ever-changing pursuit.

> *Quality teaching is more of an evolution than an attainment.*

Yes, you heard me – **pursuit!** That means it isn't finished at 3:20 at the sound of a bell, nor is it over

11

after a beginning year or after ten years. Teaching is a pursuit; until I surrendered myself to that fact, I was working under my own, self-imposed oppression, allowing others to dictate my success and also believing that I should and could do everything right and have it all together, all of the time.

I came to understand that quality teaching is more of an evolution than an attainment. I came to understand that I had to truly believe in myself, believe in what I was doing and the ways in which I was teaching. I came to understand that I needed a deeply-rooted conviction in who I was and what I felt gifted to do. I learned to rely on deep reflection to weather the ups and downs of the day and chose to cling tightly to the notion that in everything there is a lesson to be gleaned.

> *What I needed was a deeply-rooted conviction in who I was and in what I felt gifted to do.*

This book is a compilation of the lessons and reflections that came during my first few years of teaching. Yes, there are some survival tips, but it is my hope that you do far more than merely survive – that you seek to thrive in your chosen profession. That, like the great tree on the front cover of this book, your roots will go deep and you will be well nourished. That, even though you will be pruned here and there, ultimately you will bear fruit and impart nourishment and sustenance to others.

1. Your Teaching Self
Learning to Laugh and Relax the Perfectionist Within

> *Laughter helps teacher and children accept change*
> *and newness which are so important in education.*
> *A teacher who laughs and who encourages laughter is*
> *a person... who respects growth and development*
> *more than conformity.*

Dwayne E. Huebner
The Lure of the Transcendent

It was my first "real" job out of university. I had some amazing practicum opportunities and had worked as a substitute teacher for a month or so, but this was the first sign-your-name-on-the-dotted-line contract job. To say that I was keen would be a gross understatement.

The setting was a university in Japan where I was to be a lead teacher in a conversational class setting. Reasons to be nervous were numerous: a different culture, a different type of class to teach and much, much more. However, to be honest, what truly brought me the greatest amount of anxiety wasn't the content that was new or the context of the culture or my strange new surroundings; it was the fact that there were three support teachers to be in each one of my classes. The idea of having colleagues in each lesson, many who had been in that role for a few years already, frightened me to the core.

> What truly scared me was the idea of having colleagues in each lesson...

Our university language program was unique; students would receive English instruction and then get the opportunity to practise their conversational skills and the topic of the day with a native English speaker. The ratio was exceptional with one native English teacher for every three language learners. While looking back even now, their ESL model impresses me tremendously! What a commitment to immediate practice and timely feedback for students, as well as international accents and perspectives for them to engage with. But at the time, especially in the days before my first class, I was far from impressed.

The stage is now set. My first class arrived and the nervousness grew more intense. I'd always thought taking attendance was an extremely boring exercise and the surest way to lose your students within the first few minutes. According to the university, it had to be done. Creatively, I came up with a game where students wrote their names on recipe cards and ultimately, I had the cards at the front of the room and was to read them aloud. A clever way of getting them engaged as well as fulfilling my attendance requirements, so I thought.

What I didn't fully appreciate was the culture I was in, especially with regards to language and letter formation. The Japanese have three alphabets; two simpler 52 character versions and a third that boasted over 2,000 characters in common use. To me, these Kanji symbols always looked like beautiful artwork, but to my students, they read these characters from top to bottom, starting on the right side of the page and moving to the left. To complicate matters, each character had multiple brushstrokes and set orders in which said brushstrokes were to be completed. With such mastery of their own language, these students had an understanding of our alphabet, letters and the way to read them to be sure, but admittedly writing them out was often difficult for them.

Needless to say, this made my reading of their name cards only that much more complicated and my already heightened anxiety levels sky-rocketed. As I went through the cards one by one, grateful that my skirt hid my trembling knees, I imagined that with each botched name there were smirks of triumph on the faces of the veteran teachers; they truly did know more than me. Who was I to think I could come in here and be effective?

> *I imagined smirks of triumph on their faces... who was I to think I could be effective?*

It all came to a head when I said "Yakinori" and the room erupted in laughter. I had no idea what I'd said or what I'd done but the student was quick to correct his poorly shaped "u" that I'd interpreted as an "a." Oh! "Yukinori! I see! I am so sorry!" I said, trying desperately to restore order and control of the class.

16

"You just called me fried seaweed" he explained, and with that, I too joined in on the laughter. If you can't beat 'em, join 'em!

In reflecting on that day, I learned some tremendous lessons. Some of them were immediate, such as relying on computer typed attendance lists from then on. Other lessons though, have taken me longer to discover, but those first ten minutes of my very first teaching assignment taught me many things.

Firstly, don't take yourself too seriously. One time, when giving a presentation to a class in Slovakia, I wanted to use the classroom map on the wall to point to my home in Canada and, lo and behold, the darn thing came unhinged and toppled on top of me. Really, in times like that, what can you do but laugh? In another incident, I was teaching canoeing at our university pool to a group of high school students. The humid air and relaxing sound of the pool waves had attracted a good number of university students lounging in the viewing gallery and the stage was set. As I was trying to navigate my way around the big, bulky, starting-blocks and the canoe paddles on the bulkhead, all the while walking backwards so I could tell my class to enjoy their last ten minutes of free time, "WHOOSH" – in I went! I believe I even heard some applause from the viewing gallery. Those things will happen: in front of parents, administration, and most certainly in front of your students. You can't let them get to you. Just like that fateful first day on the job in Japan, I had to learn to laugh at myself. In hindsight, it was pretty funny! Come on, I did call someone "fried seaweed"!!!

> *Don't take yourself too seriously.*

A second lesson to be gleaned from that incident is that my identity is not found in perfection. There is a danger when teachers place themselves above their students, thinking of themselves as an expert or having a monopoly on knowledge. In "Finding Forester" a scholarly professor, played by F. Murray Abraham, seems to get a sort of sadistic pleasure from watching his student squirm at the authorship and meaning of a poem. When Jamal, played by Rob Brown, comes to the rescue of this poor student and challenges the professor, a recitation war ensues. It is a battle of the minds, a scuffle to see

> *Secondly, my identity is not found in perfection.*

who can name the author of this line and that line. When the student wins, the professor simply states "Get out!" He is unable to acknowledge intellect apart from his own. He is unable to see that by embracing intellectual capacity of this student, he too might learn something. In fact, the entire class could benefit by such discourse. Instead, he alone is the beholder of knowledge. He alone can disseminate truth and bestow it upon his students in the measure he so desires. In the end it is he who looks like a fool. May I never, ever seek to try to maintain a sense of perfection, a false mask of faultlessness that makes me anxious in front of the class and causes me to shut down creativity, ingenuity and desire of learning in my students.

> *There is a danger when teachers think of themselves as having a monopoly on knowledge...*

> *May I never, ever seek some mask of faultlessness that causes me to inspire less and less creativity, ingenuity and desire of learning in my students.*

I will admit, this isn't always a lesson that I have fully learned. I have to come back to this one every now and again. I remember anxiously thinking at times, "What if the students ask a question that I don't have the answer to?" I thought that if I didn't have all the answers, my credibility would be lost and I would be a poor teacher. But that was when perfection was my standard. When I learned that I am certainly not perfect, nor is anyone else for that matter, I began to loosen up. If I don't know the answer to a student's question, what a great opportunity for the class to research it together! But if I stand behind a podium, never allowing my students to inquire or bring forth deep, meaningful questions, then my teaching is really more of a farce than igniting the spark of learning within my students.

> *I thought that if I didn't have all the answers, then my credibility would be lost.*

That brings me to a third lesson buried within the seaweed incident. How I interact with my students is

> *Thirdly, how I interact with my students is evidence of the role I believe I play in their learning.*

18

evidence of the role I believe I play in their learning. Teachers always choose a role from which they instruct, and most often it is a subconscious choice based on the view they hold of their position in the path of learning. There is the expert role, whereby a teacher is the authority on a subject and is treated accordingly by his audience and his students, who are passive recipients. Another role some teachers select is the role of disseminator, whereby the teacher is a great gatekeeper and his/her role is to pass on information that he/she deems necessary; students are active recipients. At other times, teachers may act as coaches, encouraging and building skills within their students, helping them to learn. This coach dynamic marks a great shift from the other two roles. While the teacher is still in a position of greater knowledge, he/she is trying to instil the skills to acquire knowledge in his/her students. Perhaps the greatest departure is yet another role where the teacher acts as a facilitator.

> *Teachers as experts, disseminators, coaches or facilitators...*

Early on in your teaching career, you may not even be aware from which role you are teaching. Your teaching philosophy might shout out "COACH"; however, when it comes to a subject where you are not entirely familiar with the curriculum, you can resort to more of an expert/disseminator role simply out of fear or inexperience. In your first few years it is a great challenge to be conscious of which role you are teaching from, and to really determine the basic factors causing you to use the role as your platform for interacting with your students. In my desire for perfection in the classroom, I often felt that I should be in the expert role, but as I noted before, my grasp on that expertise was tenuous at best, and I soon learned that it did not foster learning in the way facilitating my classes did.

> *From which role are you teaching?*

Part of creating a safe, caring classroom environment where students are free to make mistakes has taught me another lesson - to allow that same grace to be extended towards myself. Seeing me make mistakes

> *Part of creating a safe, caring classroom is extending some of that same grace towards myself as the teacher.*

with a new language, and demonstrating an ability to laugh, persevere through it and learn from it, taught my students the skills to do that for themselves. In forgiving myself, I also gave them permission to make mistakes and to make attempts freely, without fear of mockery. Not only did that transparency help them, it also helped me and continues to help me in my classrooms today. As mentioned above, when I approach my class bearing my knowledge and perfection like a shield of armour, I am unapproachable and distant, and doomed by my own doing because I have given myself impossible standards to attain. Instead, approaching my class with open hands, realizing that no one person has a monopoly on knowledge, and that we can all learn, grow and share with one another, truly lightens the load and brings much joy to your profession.

> *Seeking perfection means that I am doomed...*

That first day of teaching in Japan served as the catalyst for other deep lessons; I will mention two more to be developed further. The first is this, that my success in teaching cannot be determined solely on the opinion of others. Secondly, teaching is not about competition. Why did I put so much power and capacity for judgement into the hands of people I never knew? Furthermore, how could I twist what was a phenomenal learning environment to be such a place of scrutiny and competition? These are much bigger fish to be

> *Why did I put so much emphasis on perfection? Could I have been partly driven by the fact I'd put so much power into the hands of others in determining my success?*

fried... not like seaweed mind you, but we'll look at them in the chapters ahead.

Reflection Questions:

1. What are some of the situations about which you can laugh easily? What are some you cannot?

2. What are you afraid your colleagues will learn about you? Why does this make you afraid?

3. How are you intimidated by colleagues? Why? What are some steps you can take to help you?

4. How are you intimidated by your students? Why? What can you do about this?

5. How could you change your standards to make your classroom more forgiving and free of stress?

Action Steps: Letting the roots go deep

- At the beginning of the year, everything is new. This is a double-edged sword; students are intrigued with the new and that curiosity can fuel learning, but novelty can also be threatening. Dr. Bruce Perry, in his article titled "Creating an Emotionally Safe Classroom", shares some tips on how to start the year off in the right direction:
    1. Keep the first few weeks of school simple: repeat the schedule and rules many times.
    2. Be predictable in your interactions with your students.
    3. Be attuned to each student's overload point – let students find some space and solitude when they seem to be overwhelmed.
    4. Keep the first challenges light and the praise heavy – confidence and pleasure come from success. Let everyone in your classroom succeed at something.[1]

- Share funny moments in class, laugh with your students, and roll with the punches when things don't go according to plan.

- If you know that certain attitudes and behaviours are causing stress and unforgiveness your classroom, begin immediately to create a safe and caring classroom environment by using some of the following strategies:
    1. Have the students help generate a list of qualities or attitudes that create a "safe" environment.
    2. Have a game plan for how you will deal with teasing or negative talk in the classroom.

---

[1] Perry, Dr. Bruce. adapted from "Creating an Emotionally Safe Classroom." http://teacher.scholastic.com/professional/bruceperry/safety_wonder.htm

Other resources:

- Wong, Harry K. and Rosemary T. Wong. ***The First Days Of School: How To Be An Effective Teacher.*** Wong Publications, 2004. ISBN-13: 978-0962936067.

This book is definitely a MUST READ in equipping teachers. From classroom routines, organizing marks, parent communication to even teacher dress; nearly every topic is covered in this comprehensive book. In reading it, you will flesh out your own educational priorities and philosophies.

- Allen n. Mendler ***Connecting with Students*** ISBN 0-87120-573-4) ASCD Publications.

Connecting with Students is a book that provides strategies for creating caring environments for students and also speaks to the need we have in society today to have greater connections within our schools. This book will help you reach out to each individual student and give you a passion for creating a warm, safe school culture that breeds acceptance and achievement.

- Julia G. Thompson ***First Year Teacher's Survival Guide: Ready-To-Use Strategies,*** Tools & Activities for Meeting the Challenges of Each School Day.. ISBN-13: 978-0787994556

This book comes highly recommended as it has an abundance of resources for teachers to help them in their first year of teaching.

2. Staffroom Climate:
From Tension to Teamwork

Competition, Comparison and Collaboration among Staff

> *The higher we soar, the smaller*
> *we appear to those who cannot fly.*
>
> - Friedrich Wilhelm Nietzsche

What is it about teaching - we can chatter on and on, all day long, encouraging our students that they are not defined by the red mark on their paper or by the comment made on the playground at recess, and yet we fail to offer ourselves the same such wisdom? We believe that in our classes, some are math-smart, some are language-smart, and others are music-smart. We encourage our students to embrace their strengths, celebrate them, and delight in them. We stress that they should not compare themselves to those around them because they are each created differently, with unique talents and abilities, and no two students are the same.

> *The messages many teachers receive are directly opposite to those they instil in their students.*

However when it comes to teachers, in many schools these lessons are lost. They are relevant to children but not to the caretakers of their education. Such words are vitally important to the self-esteem and worth of a young one, but painfully absent in the culture of the staff in many schools.

The messages many teachers receive are almost directly opposite to those we instil in our students. Many times, they come through a culture of comparison, looking at one teacher in light of the teacher they replaced, sizing up the differences and changes in programs, and comparing results from before and now. Such comparisons can occur innocently enough; a remark from a parent with regards to a slip in Johnny's spelling, because "Mrs. Smith never let him get away with such errors last year". Comparisons can come from students themselves, pitting you against the super-fun Math teacher down the hall who "never, ever, ever" assigns homework. Principals, too, can bring about comparison in discussing phenomenal field-trips in the past... the list could continue.

> *Comparisons breed nothing more but malcontent and discord.*

By definition, comparison sets out to pit one object against the other. According to Webster's Dictionary, it is "the act of comparing; an examination of two or more objects with the view of discovering the resemblances or differences".[2] Granted, when comparing, one may find many similarities, but the act of comparison itself breeds a distancing and assessing that is not healthy in human relationships. These truths even extend to the life of a family, as noted by author Elizabeth Fishel as she remarked, "Comparison is a death knell to sibling harmony." Whether it's in a family of teachers or a family of blood relatives, comparisons breed nothing more but malcontent and discord.

What if we could extract comparison from our professional environments as we do our classroom environments? What if teachers were challenged to understand one another with respect to their strengths rather than evaluating everyone with a common rubric? What if we were encouraged to shine brightly in our areas of strength, rather than hide our flaws and seek to minimize our weaknesses from the sight of others?

---

[2] "comparison." *Webster's Revised Unabridged Dictionary*. MICRA, Inc. 16 Feb. 2009. <Dictionary.com http://dictionary.reference.com/browse/comparison>.

Marcus Buckingham, a leader in management leadership, states that "the organization whose employees feel that their strengths are used every day is more powerful and more robust".[3] Instead of having people who are trained as generalists, he encourages individuality, maximizing individual strengths. He further suggests that you will "only excel by maximizing your strengths, never by fixing your weaknesses".[4] By pouring your attention and efforts into areas in which you feel gifted, you will be more excited about your work and feel more energized and successful in investing your time there. By investing time in an area that continues to be an "Achilles heel", you will feel defeated and demoralized and will often question your profession.

> *You will only excel by maximizing your strengths, never by fixing weaknesses...*

One of the greatest building blocks of success in my first few years of teaching was the notion of discovering your strengths, and building on them. Comparisons weren't really valid on our staff; we were constantly reminded that each of us is uniquely gifted and was put into our areas of specialty because it is an area of strength. In my human nature, there were most definitely times when the contrasts between myself and my colleagues were evident, when I found myself wishing I could be more like her, or teach social studies like him, but those measurements only stole joy from my day. If such appraisals were made in collusion with others, they really fractured unity on staff.

> *What if we were encouraged to shine in areas of strength, rather than hide our weaknesses?*

When comparisons are allowed to take root, a school environment becomes one of competition instead of collaboration. When everyone is seeking to come out on top when it's their turn to be

---

[3] Buckhingham, Marcus. Pg 6, <u>Now, Discover Your Strengths</u>, The Free Press, a Division of Simon & Schuster, 2001.

[4] Buckhingham, Marcus pg 26. <u>Now, Discover Your Strengths,</u> The Free Press, a Division of Simon & Schuster, 2001.

compared, information and ideas are not shared freely and professional community simply cannot exist. In an environment of comparison, my ideas become my property and my saving grace – the only thing keeping me ahead of the pack, which means I must cling to them tightly.

Teaching can be isolating. The truth is, just as iron sharpens iron, we need our colleagues just as much as they need us. When sharing a classroom dilemma with a colleague, she can offer me the support and wisdom I'd be hard-pressed to find on my own. When asking a colleague for advice about how they dealt with a rambunctious student when they taught him the previous year, I am on the fast track to success because I can begin the year with knowledge of what worked, what didn't and a better understanding of what strategies I should try. By definition, collaboration means to work together, especially in a joint intellectual effort. What other joint effort is more meaningful and more necessary than the education of our shapers of tomorrow?

> *The truth is, we need our colleagues just as much as they need us.*

> *Collaboration means to work together, especially in a joint effort.*

What a dangerous environment we create when we cannot share with one another, when we cannot work in true collaboration, and celebrate the successes of others. Assisting a fellow teacher with ideas for her science projects, or rejoicing with her when the local paper arrives to do a front page story on her class, does not minimize the work I do in *my* classroom. My work, however, will suffer as long as I see the events with regard to some great scoreboard in the principal's office, in a parents' handbook or student's binder, whereby I must accumulate as many points for my own personal glory as possible.

If my thinking remains there, in the realm of comparison and competition, I am doomed to fail as a teacher for two distinct reasons. Firstly, because there will always be someone to whom I can never measure up, whose teaching philosophy is more appealing to parents or whose energy levels are far above my own. Secondly, I will be doomed to fail simply because teaching is a job that can never be done alone, at least not done well. As teachers, we need other teachers, we need librarians, we need parental feedback, administrative support, guidance, parental encouragement and insight. It has been said that it takes a village to raise a child; it also takes a village to educate one.

> *With comparison and competition we all fail...*

> *...because there will always be someone to whom I can never measure up.*

> *...and because good teaching can never be done alone.*

The fears created in me in my first job in Japan were caused by comparison and competition. I was worried about not measuring up to the fore-knowledge other instructors had, fearful they'd scrutinize my every teaching tactic and scared they'd find out I wasn't perfect. If these attitudes had been allowed to persist, I would have drawn ever further into my shell of self-protection, and short-changed my students by delivering them a second-rate course. Furthermore, I would have short-changed myself by closing myself off to some genuinely inspiring and shaping relationships.

I especially liked what Mike Richardson said about the idea of collaboration. He states, "Being in a band is always a compromise. Provided that the balance is good, what you lose in compromise, you gain by collaboration." Collaboration can further your success, deepen your knowledge, lighten your load and refine your technique. Yes, each of us on a school staff are gifted musicians: some in areas of classroom discipline, some in curriculum, others in PR, some in drama and art, while others are gifted in science and math. Some hold the group accountable for rules and agendas

> *If collaboration is done well it can further your success, deepen your knowledge, lighten your load and refine your technique.*

while others continually seek to bring the big picture into perspective for the group as a whole. While it would be easy to free-style my own little tune and stay in my own world where I set the beat, ultimately it is in the compromise and cohesion of working together that beautiful harmony occurs and life-changing, transforming music is created.

Reflection Questions:

1. What are some areas of strength for you in teaching?

2. What are some areas you believe to be a weakness for you in teaching?

3. How can you leverage your weak areas with your strengths?

4. How is your work environment one of comparison and competition?

5. How is your work environment one of collaboration?

6. Identify areas where you could move from tension to teamwork? How will you get there?

- Focus on your strengths

- Encourage others in their areas of strengths

- Choose someone with whom to collaborate

- Learn from the past and leave it there. (Don't feel tied to do things a certain way, just because they were done that way in the past. Look at it, glean what was good, and then make it your own.)

- Self-check – if you find yourself starting to compare and contrast your achievements or your students' achievements with those of a colleague, combat those thoughts with your own self-talk. Reinforce your strengths, or the fact that you are a stronger team because you are made up of individuals who are uniquely gifted.

- Talk to your principal about collaborative sessions on staff; see if there are times during professional development days where the staff can get together in teams, based on subject matter or areas of interest, to mutually learn and work together on a common project.

- Talk to your principal regarding your teaching assignment and working towards a teaching load that is more suitable to your areas of strength.

- Act professionally – treat one another with respect, trusting their training and expertise as fellow teachers. In a study of the impact that bureaucratic structures have on professionalism in schools, it was evidenced that "the degree of teacher professionalism is related not only to the professional orientation of school leaders but also to faculty trust".[5] It was suggested that in order to develop stronger professionalism on staff, principals should consider "adopting practices that lead to strong trust among school leaders, teachers, students and parents".[6] Never underestimate the value of social gatherings with your colleagues, or team-building activities on staff. Trust is integral to professionalism and collaboration.

Another resource:

- Parker J Palmer, **The Courage to Teach: Exploring the Inner Landscape of a Teacher's Life:** ISBN-13: 978-0787910587

This book is truly one of my favourite books on teaching simply because it calls educators to look within, to not be afraid of having to know it all, but instead to teach from the passion and excitement we have within. Why do we teach? What do we believe about teaching or what do we name as best practises? This book will encourage, inspire and challenge you.

---

[5] Tschannen-Moran, Megan. "*Fostering Teacher Professionalism in Schools: The Role of Leadership Orientation and Trust.*" Educational Administration Quarterly. Vol. 45. No.2. 217 – 247. (2009).

[6] Tschannen-Moran, Megan. "*Fostering Teacher Professionalism in Schools: The Role of Leadership Orientation and Trust.*" Educational Administration Quarterly. Vol. 45. No.2. 217 – 247. (2009).

3. Dealing with Co-Workers

BEWARE of the: *Moaners, Martyrs, & Misfits*

When any fit of gloominess, or perversion of mind, lays hold upon you, make it a rule not to publish it by complaints.
~Samuel Johnson

If you have time to whine and complain about something then you have the time to do something about it.
~Anthony J. D'Angelo, The College Blue Book

"For workaholics, all the eggs of self-esteem are in the basket of work."
~Judith M. Bardwick

Prior to going out on my very first teaching practicum, we were warned as student teachers to be wary of fast friends in the various staff rooms we'd encounter that following week. While staff rooms can be intimidating and feel like a grown-up version of the high school cafeteria, the adage "choose your friends wisely" is as applicable to our upcoming circumstances as it was back then. There were certain groups, we were warned, that would be fast friends, groups that were often seeking to add numbers to their cause. We were warned that, though fast, these professional relationships would not always be fruitful or foundational.

For example, not everyone is going to be happy all of the time, but typically in each working environment there are some who simply are consistently unhappy. Let's call these the *moaners*. In each staff meeting, *moaners* focus on the negative rather than celebrate the positive. With each announcement of curricular change, the government is seeking merely to punish teachers rather than incite exciting pedagogical shifts. The paper jam in the photocopier is certainly someone setting out deliberately to ruin their day, their week and their career.

> *Moaners focus only on the negative.*

All kidding aside, it is the proverbial truth that in life there are always those who choose to see the glass as half empty. Just like you are not always going to be able to "change" your students and their opinions on a given subject, you cannot convince this group to see the glass as half full and change them. What you can do, however, is to beware of joining in on the whirlpool of negativity, because you can be assured that the current is strong and the hold is powerful. Throughout various teaching positions, I have seen this truth played out in my life. At times, I have entered a room excited and full of life regarding an idea or a challenge, and come away feeling drained and defeated as I allowed *moaners* to influence my point of view.

> *Beware of the whirlpool of negativity; the current is strong and the hold is powerful.*

You can distance yourself from the taunts that can create a snowball effect, the nit-picking that starts with a few and then grows and poisons the entire staff room and all that enter therein. Partaking in such malcontent will leave you feeling jaded at the end of the workday, dissatisfied and cynical about your chosen career, your colleagues, your students and their families. "Birds of a feather flock together," my mother always said. If you want to remain positive, surround yourself with positive people. It's as simple as that!

> *It will leave you jaded, dissatisfied and cynical...*

That said, it is not enough to only surround yourself with positive people. You must also BE a positive person.

I can remember during one teaching experience when I was complaining about a decision made by someone else and how it was affecting me in my classroom. I was annoyed that their lack of planning was infringing on my organization, and I felt justified in venting with a fellow beginning teacher. However, as I was in mid-rant, this person walked by. The knot that formed at the pit of my stomach and the worry that I experienced, fearing that this person heard me and my disgruntled opinions, were not worth the momentary benefits of venting.

> *It is not enough to surround yourself with positive people. You must BE a positive person*

In fact, the only benefit of venting is to deceptively elevate yourself, your skills and station while pointing out perceived inadequacies in others. I learned quickly that I really did not get ahead by venting; it did little to satisfy frustrations, bred only more discontent, and most certainly was far riskier than it was worth. Furthermore, there is always more than meets the eye in every situation, either personal or professional. To vent and criticize, especially from my inexperienced position, showed an audacity and lack of grace and understanding that I did not want to be known for.

> *Make a conscious effort to be consistent in dealings with every single staff member.*

I determined that my life would be authentic and tried to make a conscious effort to be consistent in my dealings with every single teacher, staff member, fellow student teacher, etc. If I gave an enthusiastic response to a new proposal by the principal, that same enthusiasm needed to be evident in my dealings with others. To shift and bad-mouth the idea would have been duplicitous, unprofessional and unfair. I have seen such people at work, saying what is most pleasing to their listener, regardless of the consistency of their lives or opinions, and they soon become unreliable and untrustworthy. Yes, the job can be hard. Yes, just as

> *You want to be known as for your positive, constancy of character. You want to be sought after on staff because you are known for your positive contributions to the team.*

in life, there will be some people that carry out duties differently than you do, or do not handle issues or tasks with as great of care as you deem necessary, but beware of voicing such complaints, lest you become known as a moaner, lacking a constancy of character that would make you a tremendously positive and sought-after, contributing member of your staff.

Another survival suggestion is to be leery of the *martyrs*, those on staff that boast of late nights, weekends marking and watching the sun rise with the photocopier. Undoubtedly, you will experience all of those things in your school year, especially if you are new on the job, if your teaching assignment has changed or if you need to invest some time on a Saturday getting a wee bit ahead (or

> *Martyrs wear the sacrifices of the job as badges of honour and identity.*

catching up!). Those necessities or realities set aside, for the sake of a healthy workplace, don't wear these tragedies as a badge of honour, walking bleary-eyed down the hallway, slopping coffee, and seeking sympathy from anyone with a listening ear.

It's easy to believe the lie that the greater the number of hours you work, the greater the success in the classroom, but it is remarkably untrue. I've been there and done that. Take my word for it − it really doesn't! Trust me!

> *The greater the number of hours you work does not equal greater success in the classroom!*

Venting or sharing the burdens of report cards with a colleague when your spouse just really doesn't understand is a good thing to do, but prefacing each lesson you teach to your Jr. High students with the number of hours it took you to create it is not professional nor praiseworthy, and it really doesn't impress them. If anything, it confirms what they may have already suspected: teachers really don't have a life outside the school!

At times, the accolades and appreciation for a beginning teacher can be few and far between. You can sometimes feel like that recognition will never come and can start to feel the need to prove that you are doing your best, more than your best actually, and start listing the sacrifices you're making in order to do your very best day in and day out. *"While I may be struggling to get my unit plan binder organized, they need to know that I was up 'til 2am laminating those game pieces for Math class"* you might think. Just as negativity can spiral out of control, so can martyrdom in this case, and one-upmanship takes on a whole new meaning as teachers boast of lesser and lesser amounts of sleep, greater workloads, and compete for the most demanding teaching schedule. It, too, is a cycle that can be extremely draining and leave you feeling tremendously dissatisfied. You can even come away feeling like you aren't sacrificing enough and throw yourself ever more into your work. You will work hard, and you will have to sacrifice, but try to be known for being industrious and hardworking by your actions, not by your words.

> *Be known for your hard work by your actions, and not by bringing attention to it by your words.*

If I could bring attention to one other group it would be one that can seem appealing when you are first on the job. I'd characterize this bunch with last-minute photocopying, boasting about teaching on the fly, and forever pushing the boundary lines of rules. These are dubbed the *misfits* – those who enjoy earning a reputation for rocking the boat and can never be accused of taking their jobs too seriously.

> *Misfits like to break the rules, and want others to rebel along with them.*

It's enticing. I'll admit – I've been attracted to them. To approach the day with a carefree spirit and nonchalance seems a lot more appealing than working hard just to get by, as I did my first year. But, when focusing on the attractive features of such a mindset, I allowed that *misfit* spirit, which is

> I allowed that misfit spirit to make me feel bad about the work I was doing.

personality for some and perhaps weak professionalism in others, to make me feel badly about the work I was doing. If I listened only to the ones with that spirit on staff, I would be left feeling that my unit planning was "too structured," my report card comments superfluous and that my exciting games or activities planned for my class were quite simply, "over the top".

It's interesting, because when considering this group, it's almost as though the social structure of Jr. High comes alive. Typically, the *misfits* appear like the popular ones on staff, and to a newbie it can seem appealing to join their ranks. However, in order to do so, you have to loosen up and perhaps give up some of the standards and expectations you have for yourself in your first years of teaching. Truthfully, no one can tell you how to do your job. I suppose administration can, but you must never allow comments made in jest

> No one can tell you how to do your job. You need to feel proud of your efforts each day.

from the *misfit* circle allow you to feel badly about working hard. You have to feel good at the front of the classroom each day. You have to feel prepared for your lessons, justified in your reporting, and proud of your efforts. Do not let others make you believe that you need to slack off simply to go along with the status quo.

In sports it is said that younger athletes have "fresh legs" because they indeed do bring more energy, youthfulness and vitality to the task at hand. In the same essential way, your newness to the profession is equally as vital, equally as integral to the team. Do not let anyone tease you for your enthusiasm. You are very well equipped, and bring to your staff unique contributions just as

44

seasoned veterans contribute their own strengths. Some day you, also, will have experience under your belt and be able to put in less hours, or not need so much prep time. You need to make sure that those decisions remain your own, and not be influenced by *misfits*. Truth be told, most of the time they work hard too; they just never let that be public knowledge!

It is difficult to enter into a school community and sometimes the staff room can seem like an intimidating place. However, by not engaging in your school community, you miss out. You pass up phenomenal resources for ideas, deny yourself a strong support team of people who truly understand what you are going through, and forgo the opportunity to be a part of a second family.

Yes, there are influences within that second family that can be dangerous as you find your feet in your profession. The *moaners*, *martyrs* and *misfits* can encumber your growth and feelings of success during your first few years. But, by entering that staff room with a head's up, by being aware of the way the attitudes and work ethic of others shape

> *Don't pass up engaging in your school community. Instead, be aware of the way the attitudes and work ethic of others shapes your own feelings.*

your own feelings towards your job, you also open yourself up to meet mentors, encouragers, and veterans on the job who will inspire and impart wisdom that will sustain you on your teaching journey. So, enjoy your school community and seek to be an active participant in it. As you do so, be thoughtful and intentional about the way you allow the attitudes and examples of others to affect your own work, and conversely the effect you are having on others.

Reflection Questions:

1. How have I allowed the attitudes and work ethics of others to influence my own outlook and behaviour at work in a negative way?

2. How have I allowed the attitudes and work ethics of others to influence my own outlook and behaviour at work in a positive way?

3. How do I feel about my interactions with other staff members? Am I proud of the way I talk about and carry out my job?

4. How can I engage more with my co-workers and be a positive force on staff?

- Have an action plan to extract yourself from negativity, either by steering the conversation in another direction or finding a task you have to do in order to leave the conversation.

- Identify those people on staff that build you up; seek frequent interactions with them and seek to be mutually encouraging.
  List them here:
    -
    -
    -
    -
    -
    -

- Let those who build you up know how meaningful their encouragement is to you in your daily activities and in your professional growth.

- From the reflection questions you've identified people/situations that do not encourage you in your profession. Seek some encounters with those people that will be focused and positive.

- When things are really tough going: perhaps your job assignment is exceedingly difficult, your co-workers are negative, and you feel as though you are getting very little support from your administration? Keep a gratitude journal in which you look for and record one nugget of goodness in each and every day. Try to actively transform the negative environment you find yourself in. Seek to be a change-maker! Having said that, also ensure that you have enough positive influence from your family, friends, and other arenas so that your well is full – so that you can pour out positivity in your work environment and not become completely depleted yourself.

Another resource:

- Joseph Ciaccio, **Totally Positive Teaching** *A Five-Stage Approach to Energizing Students and Teachers* ISBN 0-87120-880-6)

The author of this book believes that "The great teacher sees her job in a profoundly positive light. The struggling teacher, however, views teaching as more negative than positive." To that end – the aim of this book is to give educators ideas that can help them maintain more positivity in their job, which will impact their students, their achievement and therefore positively impact teachers and so forth. The positive cycle is definitely one you want to be on as a teacher.

.

4. Classroom Management

Why Bricks are Better than Elastics – Any Day!

Half of what you will accomplish in a day will be determined before you leave home. Three quarters of what you achieve will be determined before you enter the classroom door.

Harry Wong

The number one problem in the classrooms is not discipline; it is lack of authentic learning tasks, procedures and routines.

Harry Wong

I grew up being a counsellor at a summer camp. I loved it. I loved every minute of it. It became like a second home and I longed to be there, not only in the summer but also any weekend I could throughout the off-season. My love was not just for the place, but also for the full-time staff there. I respected the director a great deal; I still do, and I remember this picture he once had on the door to his office. On it stood a willow tree, bending and folding in the wind, with the caption, "Flexible branches do not break in the wind, no matter how strong the storm." It was a lesson that stuck with me through much of my part-time employment years, no matter what my job was. Whether I was counselling at camp and dealing with ten girls, twenty-four hours a day, for a week, or with the last minute changes and emergencies that would happen at the pool where I taught swimming lessons and life guarded, flexibility seemed paramount. Flexibility seemed to be a worthy goal, in everything, until I entered teacher training and began to tackle the darkest, biggest beast of the entire program – classroom management.

> *Flexible branches do not break in the wind, no matter how fierce the storm.*

My instructor wisely taught us strategies and answered questions in the classroom on campus, but it wasn't until I was in my practicum when her words rang true. I had a particular group of students in one class that had always been taught as one unit. Their program was special and with the limited enrolment in it, their class list was never altered, personalities never shuffled, power groups never dismantled. They had grown up together and had become a formidable force. They banded together in an "us" versus "you" mentality and were infamous for sending teachers to nervous breakdowns or stress leaves.

It was in that very class that my university professor was scheduled to observe and evaluate my performance, and what an experience it was! She'd seen me with other tough groups, but readily admitted that this one was an exception. She challenged me to be strong, to be like a brick wall

> *The brick wall is built firmly and solidly, outlining boundaries.*

right from the start. If I didn't – the only other option was to be an elastic band, one that would be stretched and stretched until one day I'd snap.

There are basically two options when it comes to classroom management. The brick wall is built piece by piece, firmly and solidly, and outlines boundaries wherein students and teachers alike can interact. Each party knows what is expected and accordingly can have more

> *Teachers and students alike know what is expected. They can interact within the clearly defined boundaries.*

freedom and flexibility because of the clearly defined boundaries.

On the other hand, an elastic approach occurs when a rule or procedure is set in place, and then stretched. It is stretched by letting one person get away with breaking it "just for today". It is stretched further when the procedures become ambiguous, or applied liberally to certain students and not to other s. The interesting thing about elastic is that tension builds as it is stretched further and further. To push the analogy even more, as a teacher, if I feel my policies and procedures are not being respected, there is great tension and in that tension I can often overreact, bringing down consequences like a hammer and leaving students only more confused about classroom expectations. Elastic can only be stretched so far before it snaps and causes all kinds of injuries. Injury comes to the student-teacher relationship as students deal with the hurt of being strictly disciplined despite the fact that they never quite knew where the lines were drawn. Further injury is caused to the self because many of us experience moments of extreme doubt in our chosen profession, as we see so clearly in this that we failed to get it right.

> *The elastic approach is when a rule is stretched, and boundaries become ambiguous and uncertain.*

> *Rules are stretched, tempers snap and respect relationships are damaged because the boundary lines were never clearly drawn.*

Despite the injuries, the elastic approach can seem most appealing. Flexibility seems paramount; gaining the students' trust and building relationships seem like worthy goals, especially at the beginning of a school year. I faced this crisis my first day of school in my first Canadian, full-year teaching assignment. I had written my grade six students a welcome letter, and the assignment for the afternoon was to reply to me, using the same format I had outlined in my letter. I had even created side tabs to my letter, which highlighted the featured elements that their letter had to have. The results were disparaging. Only a fraction was up to specifications and for those who had met all criteria, they had not met it well. I was faced with a choice. I could discuss with the class my disappointment at their

> *Flexibility seems most appealing on first glance.*

lack of effort and attention to assignment specifics but be flexible, let them off with the promise that I knew they could do better and would be anticipating better next time around, or I could make a point. I could reinforce my brick wall right then and there, first day.

Reinforce I did. The second day of school began with the entire class re-doing their first assignment as it should be completed, with proper effort and attention to the assignment specifics. Did the lesson work? Yes, for that day and for the next few weeks. Then challenges began to arise and the students seemed to want to stand at the edge of that brick wall boundary and test just how firm those boundaries were, just how set that mortar truly was. During that time I felt like a nag, but I continued reaffirming because I knew that it was worth it. It was, in fact, essential that I be a stickler for the rules for a week or two every semester because it would set the stage for the rest of the year. If I could clearly define the boundaries and

> While I felt like a nag, I kept reaffirming my brick wall boundaries because I knew that it was worth it.

defend them vigorously, I could set up a classroom climate that was consistent and conducive to learning.

I haven't always abided by this strategy. In a particularly tough language arts class, I had a group of rowdy students that learned quickly that my threats of sending them to the principal's office were never acted upon and simply resulted in greater threats. That class had the upper hand and they managed me for a few painful weeks of my student practicum.

> With some students I am great at being a brick wall, but with others I can be extraordinarily elastic.

In another circumstance I was painfully aware of the fact that with some students, I was great at being a brick wall, but with others, I was extraordinarily elastic. A father of a very well-behaved student talked to me about the fact that his daughter was really struggling with being teased by a young man in class. This father was frustrated with the seemingly endless second chances this student had, and the fact that there seemed to be no consequences. I realized that in an effort to give mercy to a student with a painful history and struggling home situation, I had been far too flexible and created a situation of real injustice. While discipline must always be done considering the

> *The balance of grace and justice – to ensure that graciousness doesn't affect the validity of the brick wall for the entire class.*

student, by no means can everyone be painted with the same brush; I had erred more on the side of mercy than on justice, and the brick wall I had really worked hard to achieve for the entire class was losing its strength because of it.

Some students who crave justice need to learn mercy, while those who take advantage of mercy need to learn the lines of boundary and consequence. Through my interaction with that father, I learned that often students can have a warped perception of the discipline being administered and naturally, can have an inflated need for justice. I also learned that when some students are repeatedly given second chances, sometimes by multiple teachers in a day, the perceived system of reward and punishment a teacher has in place begins to lack credibility. Because of the breakdown in this system and its accompanying lack of trust, students will turn to other authority figures to assist in restoring a balance of justice. I was painfully aware of the fact that I had been indulgent and brought the tumbling of my brick wall about by my own means.

> *As a teacher, by admitting things had gone awry and re-evaluating our "bricks" together was a turning point*

Was it all for loss? Not at all! Call it going back to basics, or wiping the slate clean, but by starting anew as a class we could revisit the bricks that constituted our wall in the first place. We could discuss, as a whole, which rules were fair, which were unnecessary, and which were needed to maintain a safe and just classroom environment for learning. By admitting that things had gone a bit awry, by honestly speaking to the students about the fact that justice needed to be restored, a real turning point was reached. It was as though the veil had been lifted from what we all knew, but no one was talking about. These grade seven students truly wanted a healthy classroom environment, even the ones who had stepped out of line. On the whole, the students appreciated that I could admit that I was not perfect. They also appreciated another opportunity, now that they'd experienced half a

> *They appreciated the opportunity to set realistic guidelines and expectations...*

year in Jr. High, to set classroom guidelines that were realistic, and standards that were attainable. I was able to change course mid-stream, re-align our standards and invite them into a new level of accountability for themselves and their peers, as well as for me.

As teachers, we can sometimes be caught up in our legacy, in thinking of our lasting imprint on the lives of our students. What kind of imprint are we leaving? What am I, as an individual teacher, known for? What am I remembered for? As tempting as it is to be known as "the nice teacher", to be remembered for being accommodating and adaptable, when it comes to classroom management I would rather be known for being firm yet fair, unyielding yet understanding. I would rather be known as the teacher who had rules and procedures in

> *While we all want to be known as the nice teacher, I'd rather be known for being firm yet fair...*

place and they may have seemed tough, but you always knew what to expect. To me, that is why I'll take the bricks and mortar approach over elastics, any day.

1. Looking back, can I identify areas when I have acted more like elastic and could have used more of a brick and mortar approach?

2. Can I identify students or circumstances when my flexibility with rules has injured the teacher-student trust relationship?

3. How will a brick wall approach affect my rule-followers? How will it affect my most disruptive students?

4. What is going to be non-negotiable in my classroom? What are the rules and standards that will serve as my brick wall, to outline proper classroom behaviour in my room?

Other things to consider:
   -What do I do about late students?

   -What do I do about students insulting one another in class?

   -What do I do about late homework?

   -What do I do about cheating?

   -What do I do about apparent lack of effort on assignments?

   -At what point do I get parents involved?

-Where am I going to post my classroom standards for my students to see?

-What positive incentive program do I have that's going to enforce students who stay within the brick wall standards?

-What am I going to do with repeat offenders?

-Is there a way my school's existing discipline policy can enhance my individual classroom management plan? Or, can I discuss this with my colleagues and administration team and see about collaboration and consistency here?

5. How do students in my classroom know what the non-negotiables are? How are they held accountable to these?

Action Steps: Letting the roots go deep

- Take an honest assessment of your current classroom management practices.

- Make clearly defined boundaries for your classroom and post them, photo-copy them, make them available in as many ways possible so that students know what is expected of them, and what the anticipated consequences will be.

- Connect with your administration team and/or colleagues and ensure that your personal policies line up with those of your school and co-workers.

- Actively, each and every day, enforce your brick wall rules – even if it's student "A" who never makes a mistake, or student "B" who consistently tests the limits. Decide to outline the boundaries and defend them rigidly.

Other Resources:

- Robert J. Marzano, Barbara B. Gaddy, Maria C. Foseid, Mark P. Foseid and Jana S. Marzano ***Handbook for Classroom Management that Works*** ISBN: 978-1-4166-0236-1

A phenomenal guidebook to research based ideas for classroom management techniques. It is a very large read, but will offer some great inights.

- Doug Lemov, ***Teach Like a Champion: 49 Techniques that Put Students on the Path to College***, ISBN-13: 978-0470550472

A more concise book that offers training on techniques that will truly make life easier in the classroom. The book comes with a DVD with segments demonstrating the techniques.

5. The Essence of Teaching:
Truly Making an Impact

'It is my personal approach that creates the climate. It is my daily mood that makes the weather... I possess tremendous power to make a child's life miserable or joyous. I can be a tool of torture or an instrument of inspiration. I can humiliate or humour, hurt or heal. In all situations, it is my response that decides whether a crisis will be escalated or de-escalated and a child humanised or dehumanised.'

Haim Ginott
Teacher and child: A book for parents and teachers, 1995

For many students school is a refuge. It is a place of structure, love, routine and affirmation that they may rarely get at home. For others, it is just the opposite. Perhaps they may have a highly loving, structured home-life and find that school is a place of ridicule, difficulty and failure. For students at both ends of the spectrum, and all in between, you as their teacher become a very essential part of their days. The ways in which you handle, view, affirm, discipline, praise and teach, deeply impact the lives of your students. This is not said to weigh down your already heavy workload, but to foster a deep appreciation and respect for the special role you have in the lives of your students.

> *The ways in which you handle, view, affirm, discipline, praise and teach, deeply impact the lives of your students.*

It is essential to not diminish the role a teacher plays in the lives of their students for two reasons: for the student's sake as well as the teacher's sake. Firstly, teachers will take greater ownership and care of their teaching if they believe it has meaningful impact. The value derived from the work of their hands has a tremendous correlation to their own satisfaction on the job. The deeper the meaning teachers attribute to their work, the greater their efforts will be at teaching and the more satisfied they will be in their jobs. Secondly, students are impacted by a healthy respect of the potential influence a teacher can have because their teachers will seek to have meaningful lessons and conversations, and essentially not give up on them.

> *The deeper the meaning teachers attribute to their work, the greater their efforts will be and the more satisfaction they will receive.*

It is crucial that teachers seek to connect well with their students. Many students will not remember the intricacies of Grade Eleven Algebra or the deeper meaning behind Shakespeare's sonnets, but they will remember how you made them feel about themselves, their capacity for learning, and their dreams for the future. While they may put on a tough persona and act as though they could care less, the opposite is true. Behind the veil of makeup, piercings, rude language and attitudes that speak disdain for you and the whole world, against all establishments and status quo, resides a child desperately seeking love and affirmation, urgently in search of significance and meaning in this world. You, as a teacher, have been given a mighty, mighty privilege to often be able to see through those cracks, to be given, at times, entry into that deep, inner recess and to have the ability to impact your students at the core of their deepest needs.

> *It is crucial that teachers seek to connect well with their students.*

Following are some ideas to help you foster strong relationships with your students and seek to truly impact their lives in a positive way:

• *Introductions:*

I well remember a university professor in the education department who greeted everyone at the door with a firm handshake, asking us our names and welcoming us to his class. After all forty of us had arrived and were seated in the classroom, he proceeded to recall all of our names, one by one. The order in which we'd entered or the random seats we'd selected did not seem to matter. He'd been studying our pictures taken by the department and, being the good professor that he was, knew the importance of building connections with his students. He didn't want to waste a

> *We each had a singular identity with him... what a difference that made!*

single day in establishing that rapport, so immediately set a tone of connection, understanding and significance. We were not simply one of forty anonymous faces in the crowd; we each had a singular identity to him. What an impact that had on all of us! Whatever the sizes of your classes, or the number of different blocks you teach, seek to know your students' names. Make this something you study and prioritize above all else at the beginning of each new term or new school year. It provides instant connection; it can also alleviate discipline issues in the future.

• *Meaningful Relationships:*

Just as it is important to have solid introductions, to make names a priority in your classroom, it is important that the development of strong relationships with your students doesn't end there. Seek to add meaning to your relationships with each and every individual student. Notice the little things. A Motocross logo on a boy's shirt is an open invitation to ask about his love of the sport; a pretty bow in a girl's hair is an invite to compliment her. Asking about how the basketball game went last night, or a ballet recital on the weekend, are ways of building meaning into relationships with your students. By taking an avid interest in their lives, your students know that you care, first and foremost. They may also care about what you know and what you have to share in your teaching because you have shown them the same courtesy.

Just as we adults can sense when someone is asking how we are doing, simply just to ask the question and not truly to hear the answer, your students have the same understanding and ability to read authenticity. Ask how they are doing and sincerely care about the answer. Often we as teachers can be so goal-oriented that we are forever on a mission – off to the photo-copier or to a meeting – that we miss opportunities for connections. I encourage you to slow down, look for those opportunities and make time for them. If possible, build them into your classroom routine if you have a home room. Take the time to share, to laugh, to talk with the students; don't forget to take the time to listen.

> *Knowing names provides instant connections and taking an avid interest in their lives shows that you care...*

One method I found that works very well with my students is "B-mail". It is like e-mail, but it is directed to me, Miss B and therefore it is "B-mail". It is a small journal where students can write to me and I respond to them. How well it works depends on how long it takes for me to return the journals and how much time I devote to writing back to them. For the students who are not as verbal as others, this is a way I have been able to connect with them. For others, it is important I stop them in the hallway and talk with them verbally. You will have to find whatever works with your personality and the personality of your students, but find that meaningful connection on a daily basis. If possible, try to be aware of the quiet, shy kids that often can sneak under your radar. In an effort to make sure that no one feels uncared for or overlooked in my classroom, I sometimes take time during the day to glance at my class list and ask, "Have I connected with him yet today or this week?"

> *Seek meaningful connections with each of your students on a daily basis.*

• *Power for Positivity:*

As I mentioned before, our students come from incredibly complex and diverse backgrounds. For some, school is another arena for

> *Emphasize the positive as much as possible.*

success; their parents are actively involved in various committees. Their foundations for life are secure, stable and strong. However, with the disintegration of many marriages, the varied stresses on families, and the growing power of media in the minds of kids, our students come to us desperately needing

some goodness infused into their days. For some it is a science project that they can get excited about, and for others it's being in an environment where they are free to make mistakes without the fear of physical punishment.

While we need to keep discipline in the classroom, we can be a · major force for good in the lives of our students. We can add much value to their days by focusing on the positive, by getting them excited about their lives, about learning, and about their unique talents and gifts.

• *Absolution:*

Absolution is defined by Random House Dictionary as the "act of absolving; a freeing from blame or guilt; release from consequences, obligations, or penalties".[7] In a traditional sense, it is a word attributed to the religious theology of proclaiming divine forgiveness of sins to someone who was penitent. In other words, it is forgiving someone who has asked to be forgiven or who is seeking forgiveness.

What an essential component to our classroom teaching – to keep short accounts with our students and allow them the chance each day and each period for a fresh start. If a student had a terrible morning, broke all the rules, and experienced the consequences of

---

[7] "absolution." *Dictionary.com Unabridged (v 1.1)*. Random House, Inc. 30 Mar. 2009. <Dictionary.com http://dictionary.reference.com/browse/absolution>.

those actions, it is very healing for the student to know that he/she can start fresh in the afternoon. It is empowering for them to know that they do not have to be defined by their past mistakes, but that they have the power to dictate what the afternoon will be like, based on their behaviour.

> *Keep short accounts, allowing students a fresh start.*

With this in mind, it is important to give each student a fresh start as often as you can. While it is beneficial to talk to teachers from previous years, try to ensure that their stories and anecdotes do not influence your perceptions of your new class in September.

What about those students who do not seek forgiveness? What about those who wear their long list of offences like a badge of honour? They also need that fresh start. They also need to learn that they can command their future, that they can order their course and create a more positive direction with each step they take and choice they make.

• *Compassion:*

Do you remember what it was like to not be invited to someone's birthday party in grade two? Or to be made fun of for your outfit in Jr. High? Or to not be picked for the soccer team or to have your teacher mock your answer on a test in front of the class?

We've all been through similar experiences. Keeping them in mind will help us as teachers to be more compassionate with our students. I have discovered that sometimes sharing some of these incidents from my past has helped my own students deal with their present struggles. It shows them that a dreadful week in school where they feel as if their lives are going to end isn't as catastrophic

> *Remember the trying times you yourself went through. It can help you put yourself in your student's shoes and exhibit compassion*

as they think it might be; just as I experienced something similar and pulled through, so can they.

In my university English Language Arts class my professors, who team-taught, tried to teach us English major students how to best impart our love of literature and language to students of all ages. One day, we were given a spelling test – an impossible twenty-word test with the weirdest, most complicated spelling patterns the English language could throw at you. Not only were these words hard, they were inconsequential, words we'd never used, like "sarsaparilla." Anxiety grew in our adult hearts as the test continued, and it quadrupled as we were instructed to hand over our sheet of paper to our neighbour beside us for marking purposes. As if that wasn't humiliating enough, we had to call out our scores to the teachers and they wrote down our grades.

Although what they did breaks all types of "Privacy of Information Acts", that wasn't the purpose of the activity. The re-creation of a very standard classroom practice (let's hope **formerly** standard practice) placed us in the position of our students and caused us to experience the fear with such difficult testing, the dread of someone else seeing our incompetencies when we were asked to peer-mark, and the humiliation of having to vocalize our performance in front of everyone. This lesson taught me the importance of relevant testing, proper marking procedures, privacy rules, etc. Most of all, it taught me compassion. It taught me to never forget what it is like to be a student, to be vulnerable and exposed. It also taught me to use that compassion to continue to desire to learn and to feel valued.

> *Never forget what it is like to be a student.*

To be compassionate is often viewed as being "soft". To be a teacher that gives an extension, or allows for a re-write can be viewed by some as being the elastic band. If you are stretching rules and standards, one day you will snap, break and come down hard to re-establish order. But what if compassion was part of the order? What if students could know that your classroom wasn't all about getting it right on a certain day of the week, but instead, practising, learning, failing, and learning more. As a result, when they feel confident and ready, their knowledge and understanding will be showcased.

There is an exciting movement in the arena of assessments, distinguishing assessments *for* learning, from assessments *of* learning. This new movement departs from the "too bad, so sad" mentality, which much of our traditional testing communicates, towards a more compassionate and equipping model which allows students to receive greater feedback, more focused practice, resulting in opportunities to show their learning. The move towards more compassionate teaching is an exciting one.

• *Try, Try Again:*

One of the greatest lessons you can give your students is the understanding that life is not about getting it perfect on the first attempt. Unfortunately, our traditional methods of testing and mark-taking often affirm that theory, but as I noted above, that is changing for the better.

> *Waiting until everything is perfect before making a move is like waiting to start a trip until all the traffic lights are green.*
>
> *- Karen Ireland*

I love the point made by the quote above. It demonstrates the impossibility of having everything perfect before beginning a task. Similar logic can creep into the minds of our students: the desire to never show their work before it is perfect, or the desire to never write down a wrong answer and consequently they never speculate, infer or surmise.

Part of the problem is the fact that students are often praised for "being smart" rather than for their efforts in struggling through the learning process. Is a student who achieves a 90% on the test better than one who fails miserably and proceeds to relearn, study and achieve 93% on a test of similar difficulty and similar concepts a week later?

Failure is okay! Does my teaching practice live up to that belief? Do I allow my students to grow?

70

If we do not give our students opportunities to try again, many can simply give up on school and give up on life. They simply are a "C" student; they simply are not smart. This is what many in the educational psychology world have termed a "fixed mindset" – the notion that ability is something unchangeable.

> *Intelligence is not fixed...you can grow and achieve through hard work!*

The greatest lesson we can impart to our students is to teach them that their intelligence isn't something that is fixed. They can achieve what they desire through hard work, through overcoming obstacles and through failing, getting back up and trying it again.

Carol Dweck, a professor of Psychology at Stanford University, states "the key isn't ability; it's whether you look at ability as something inherent that needs to be demonstrated or as something that can be developed."[8]

Dweck has developed a theory on what separates learners into "helpless versus mastery-oriented". She explains these two classes of learners deeper in stating:

> "I realized that these different types of students not only explain their failures differently, but they also hold different "theories" of intelligence. The helpless ones believe that intelligence is a fixed trait: you have only a certain amount, and that's that. I call this a "fixed mind-set." Mistakes crack their self-confidence because they attribute errors to a lack of ability, which they feel powerless to change. They avoid challenges because challenges make mistakes more likely and looking smart less so..."

---

[8] Carol Dweck, *The Effort Effect,* Stanford Magazine, March/April 2007.

"The mastery-oriented children, on the other hand, think intelligence is malleable and can be developed through education and hard work. They want to learn above all else. After all, if you believe that you can expand your intellectual skills, you want to do just that. Because slipups stem from a lack of effort, not ability, they can be remedied by more effort. Challenges are energizing rather than intimidating; they offer opportunities to learn. Students with such a growth mind-set, we predicted, were destined for greater academic success and were quite likely to outperform their counterparts."[9]

[9]Dweck, Carol. "The Secret to Raising Smart Kids." Scientific American. November, 2007.

The "Fixed vs. Growth Mindset" theory is explained further by the image below:

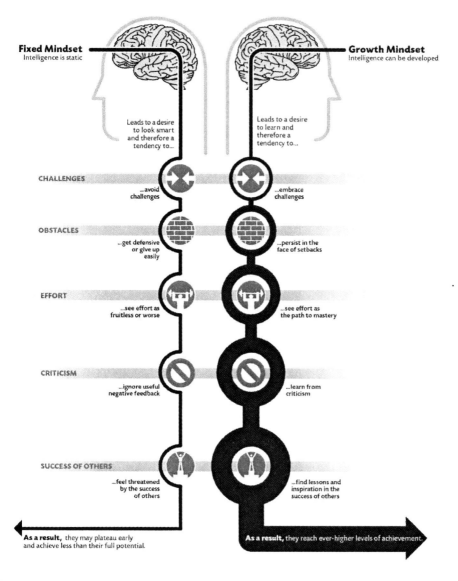

TWO MINDSETS – Carol S. Dweck, Ph.D. - Graphic by Nigel Holmes

Reprinted with permission

s teachers, we can also learn from the different mind-sets. If we
elieve that we simply are the kind of teacher that we are, and that we
an not affect change in our practice, we will avoid obstacles and

challenges and remain very much the same as we were when we first graduated. Rather, if we embrace the growth mind-set, not only for our students but also for ourselves, we will find new challenges invigorating and will actually develop, expand and refine our teaching practice.

Throughout the chapter, ideas were given about how to develop strong relationships with your students in order to create the greatest impact on the future. These ideas form an acronym that spell "I-M-P-A-C-T":

I - Introductions: never forget the power of knowing someone's name, having a strong first impression and making them feel welcome.

M – Meaningful Relationships: seek to connect in a meaningful manner with each of your students on a regular basis. Zero in on hobbies, likes, and dislikes, and make a point of acknowledging them.

P – Power for Positivity: Seek to always infuse the good into the lives of your students, whether it be respect for others, the earth, or for themselves.

A – Absolution: Simply put, remember to forgive – to give your students the opportunity often to start afresh. They need to know that they are not tied to past wrongs, but they can make constructive choices that will have positive consequences.

C – Compassion: Don't ever forget what it was like to be a student; try to use that knowledge to better structure your lessons, your tests and your discipline. Seek to love your students and let that love be evident in how you treat them.

T – Try, Try Again: Teach your students that a grade is never final, nor a judgement on their abilities, but an opportunity to learn more, work harder, and achieve greater things.

1. Do I believe that, as a teacher, I have an impact on the lives of my students?

2. In what ways am I currently impacting the lives of my students? Think hard and list them all.

3. In what ways do I want to impact the lives of my students? Dream big and list as many as you can.

4. What can I do in each area of the IMPACT acronym to foster stronger relationships with my students and have the greatest impact?

I - Introductions:	
M – Meaningful Relationships:	
P – Power for Positivity	
A – Absolution:	
C – Compassion:	
T – Try, Try Again:	

5. Reflect on the following:

Ways I promote a "fixed mind-set" belief in my classroom:	Ways I can change to promote more of a "growth mind-set":

6. Find a colleague or teaching partner to help you reflect on the contents of this chapter and the changes you desire to make in your classroom. Ask them to help you set tangible, measurable goals as you desire to promote more of a "growth mind-set" environment. List at least three of the goals you've determined below:

A) Goal:

Strategies to get there:

I will know I have achieved this when:

B) Goal:

Strategies to get there:

I will know I have achieved this when:

C) Goal:

Strategies to get there:

I will know I have achieved this when:

Action Steps: Letting the roots go deep

- Have a class list in your binder that is simply for memory association so that you can write quick adjectives or memory-markers to help you not only remember the names of your students but also their affinities. Ensure that this is not an anecdotal list for behaviours – that should be kept somewhere out of sight and private, but make this list your cheat sheet for connections. E.g. Write down that Joey plays basketball, that Suzie just had a new baby sister, or that talking about video games makes Dan's eyes come alive.

- Be ready for your class, rather than running to the photo-copier or assembling material at your desk, so that you can stand at the doorway and greet your students as they enter the room. Similarly, it is important to take some time to properly wish your students well at the end of class. Just standing by the door and ensuring each student looks you in the eye as you wish them well can be meaningful, even for older students. That eye-to-eye contact takes away the feelings of anonymity and instantly makes students feel significant and noticed.

- Curb negative comments in the classroom, phrasing requests in a positive, not negative, way. This is difficult, but aim to be an optimistic light in the classroom. Endeavour to keep a stressful night's sleep, a fight at home, or a rough commute, from tainting your interactions with your students. If you happen to be a little sharp, excuse yourself, ask for forgiveness and explain to your students that you're a little irritable today, and could use some extra cooperation and understanding. That kind of acknowledgement teaches them that it's okay, everyone has bad days, but you don't have to take it out on others.

- Enter into professional discussions with colleagues and administrators regarding learning opportunities on assessment, especially along the ideas of assessing **for** learning, and assessment **of** learning. Any further investigation into this topic and additional reading about growth and fixed mind-sets will transform your practice and have tremendously positive impacts on the lives of your students.

Another resource:

- Edited by Robert Sornson and James Scott **Teaching and Joy** , ISBN-13: 978-0-87120-271-0

The editors of this book have created a collection of stories, articles and anecdotes to "reinforce the perspective that great learning and great teaching can occur only in an atmosphere of love, clear purpose, and commitment. To us, that describes an atmosphere of joy." Through reading this book you will be reminded of your great calling as a teacher and the great joy to be found in our profession.

6. Life/Work Balance
Tire-Pressure Monitoring System

*The National Commission on Teaching and America's Future
has calculated that nearly a third of all new teachers
leave the profession after just three years and that after five years
almost half are gone.*

NY Times[10]

*Due to burnout, about 30 percent of new primary and
secondary teachers leave the profession within five years.*
(Archer, 1999; Boreen, Niday, & Johnson, 2003).

One of the greatest reasons why teachers leave the profession is burnout or fatigue. Typically, teachers enter the profession because they love their subject matter, they love working with children, or they love the school environment. But what people rarely realize when they come into the profession is the all-encompassing demands on their time, the ways in which the job can be limitless, and the fact that rewards are not always tangible. Teacher burnout is a very real thing, and something that you need to be aware

> *Teacher burn-out is a very real thing.*

of as you enter the profession. I wasn't quite so aware. I knew it existed and I knew it was something to be careful of, but this was my dream job. I'd always dreamed of being a teacher – how could I ever find it unsatisfying or depleting, even for a moment?

I remember one November day, after my first round of report cards, where I had more marks in my mark book than some

---

[10] NY Times, Parker-Pope, Tara, Teacher Burnout? Blame the Parents, January 2008. http://well.blogs.nytimes.com/2008/01/02/teacher-burnout-blame-the-parents/

teachers had in a year. At the same time, I was also trying to reinvent the wheel, not only once, but five times over with every single class I was given. I'd been trying to do phenomenal year plans for each one of my new classes, but being new to the school and the grade levels, everything was therefore new.

I was losing steam, losing focus and losing the joy I had most days in September and October. Student engagement in my classes was down and I was finding myself stepping into the role of disciplinarian more and more. This resulted in receiving less and less satisfaction from my work – all classic, tell-tale signs of approaching burn-out. Needless to say, my administration team were concerned.

One night I left my work at school and enjoyed a totally "me" night. The next day, I was refreshed and revived. In a Social Studies History class, I knew I was far more animated and energetic in the classroom. It wasn't that the format of my lessons or its content changed, but my delivery had changed. I hadn't stayed up all night making a game board to suit the topic, or agonizing over attention-grabbing questions that would start the class off

> *Because I was refreshed and had taken care of myself, my delivery in class had changed and the class was far more successful!*

just right. Instead, I actually enjoyed my job that day. What added even more to the pleasure of that class was the fact that I had fewer discipline issues, simply because the students were engaged and interested.

The problem was that I'd allowed my tires to go flat in some areas, and bulge in other areas. I'd skipped aerobic classes at my gym because the next day's lessons were too important. My times of prayer, journaling and contemplation that are so life-giving to me were easily squeezed out and deemed a luxury I simply could not afford in my first year of teaching. I was new to the city, with family and friends a distance away; therefore I had few people in my life who could challenge me with regards to my overwork.

In order to keep moving along the road of life, your tires must be balanced; the pressure in each quadrant must be equal for you to enjoy a smooth ride. So often, I was neglecting all other quadrants and putting all of my energies into my schoolwork. Soon, my health was suffering, relationships dwindled and my spiritual life became parched.

> *In order to keep moving along life's road well, your tires must be balanced.*

> *My lesson plans and nicely kept binders have an expiry date; someday they will be obsolete and be recycled.*

To borrow another analogy, it was as though all my eggs were in one basket – my professional basket. I was expending little effort and energy in any other area and was most certainly on the fast track to burnout.

Another tangible lesson at the same time resulted from some housekeeping that I did in my classroom; I sorted and sifted through a myriad of old lessons and materials left to me by others in my position. As I perused binders in which someone had clearly invested countless hours, I proceeded to recycle them because the curriculum had changed, the textbooks were now obsolete or the style of teaching did not align with mine. The lesson was starkly obvious. As I tossed another handful into the bin, I realized that in five to ten years, someone may very well be doing the exact same thing to my binders. As much as I love them, as much time as I invest in them and get excited about creating exciting year plans, they too have an expiry date. They, also, will be obsolete someday. Neither are they protected from changes in pedagogy and practice.

My vice-principal had joined in the chorus with my principal. He echoed my principal's concerns and, being new to the school himself, he could empathize with the circumstances I was facing. He also found himself teaching many new courses. He suggested that I not try to inject newness into everything, all at once. Instead, he suggested concentrating on one spoke of the wheel at a time. He recommended I invest time in revamping only one subject each month, or one unit at a time, not five all at once. Rather than spreading my limited attention to five or ten different projects and thereby giving only partial attention to each, the advice was to pull back and focus only on one or two at a time. That was excellent advice. His words were another piece of my teaching journey that helped me put boundaries where needed and get off the fast track to burnout.

Pick one subject, one project, one area to develop at a time.

By intentionally seeking balance, you secure for yourself some staying-power in the teaching profession.

How do we achieve balance? It seems that question is applicable not only in teaching. Its elusive quest does not discriminate by profession, age, sex, or experience. So that's it? It's just a fact of life, in many professions, and just a given that we'll always have to fight for balance?

Rather than succumb to defeat and go through your teaching career moving forward inefficiently, bumping and bruising on uneven tires, know this to be true: balance is fittingly a worthy pursuit. Just because it is difficult to achieve and might look different for each person you meet, it does not mean it isn't worth the effort to attain it. It is in the striving, the aiming for the target that you build for yourself some boundaries, some checks and balances and accountability partners to assist you. By intentionally seeking balance, you secure for yourself some staying-power in the teaching profession. By becoming a reflective practitioner, one who evaluates often, you set yourself up to beat the odds of burnout.

It is easy to think that this workaholic behaviour is a must for your first few years of teaching and that once you have it all figured out, you will be fine. I believed this for a time, thinking that all the hours I spent would pay off down the road. Although there is some truth in that the job does get easier, the danger lies in the fact that by doing so you will create habits and attitudes towards your work that will be hard to break, even if your load gets easier or more familiar.

> *The job gets easier with experience, but workaholic attitudes and habits created in your first years in the profession often will not change, no matter how many years on the job.*

Either go to school early or stay late, but do not do both. Furthermore, as exciting as it is to see all the new and fantastic professional development opportunities come your way, take them in stride.

Invest some time in balance. Create for yourself a tire-pressure monitoring system and get someone who you love to help you stick to it. Blowouts on the highway are never pretty nor safe and they are, in fact, irreversible. Once ruptured, the pieces are impossible to recover.

Reflection Questions:

1. Think through what takes up your time in the quadrants of your life :
   - ○ In the second column – "What it IS currently??? like" – list all the activities that currently use up your time in the four areas: Physical, Spiritual, Relational and Professional.
   - ○ In the second column, underline those things that are necessities – that cannot be given up.
   - ○ What would you LIKE each quadrant of your life to look like? What activities would you like to see characterize that section? Note them in the third column.

	The way it is NOW:	The way I would like it to be:
Physical		
Spiritual		
Relational		
Professional		

2. Complete the chart below, noting honestly how much of your unstructured/free time you invest into each component of your life wheel. After indicating how many hours each quadrant has of your time, give a rough estimate of the corresponding percentage that component has of your free time each week.

	time / week	% of your week
Physical		
Spiritual		
Relational		
Professional		

3. Are you shocked... surprised... dismayed... pleased... by the answers above?

4. How can you have a more balanced time allotment?

5. Work boundaries: Barring exceptional times like report cards, parent-teacher interviews and the first and last few weeks of school, these are my boundaries when it comes to work:

- Time to go into work

- Time to leave work

- Time to spend on prep or marking at home

- Turn-around time on assignments

6. Who are your boundary-keepers? Who are the people you've invited into your life who are going to help you stay committed to your work boundaries?

Action Steps: Letting the roots go deep

- Go in early or stay late – but don't do both. Contact your boundary-keepers and commit to certain working hours with them.

- Choose an area of focus for the month – a subject or a project where you can focus your energies, rather than trying to juggle all kinds of classes and commitments.

- Review the charts in the reflection section often: look back at what eats up most of your time, and consider where you would really like to invest your time. Ensure that you are taking action steps to realize your dreams and goals.

Another resource:

- Mary Rose O'Reilley , ***The Garden at Night: Burnout and Breakdown in the Teaching Life*** ISBN-13: 978-0325008486

This book comes highly recommended, and offers words of encouragement as O'Reilley challenges teachers to live beyond the daily grind. In the words of my favourite educational author,

"I cannot imagine a person who would not find guidance in what Mary Rose says for all the far reaches of being alive, well beyond the work we do and the places where we do it.
- Parker J. Palmer, author of *The Courage to Teach*

7. Dealing With Parents
Standing Tall – Even With a Parent's Call

*Criticism, like rain, should be gentle enough to nourish a man's growth
without destroying his roots.*

Frank A. Clark

Like a scene in a Mr. Bean movie, my classroom phone took on a
life of its own and began to become, very unwillingly, the object of
my obsession. The sense of relief I felt when I saw only the date
and time on the call display was enormous, but not nearly as big as
the dread I would feel in the pit of my stomach with the words
"MESSAGE FOR YOU" displayed.

I dialled the code, entered my password, waited for my messages
to be retrieved, and held my breath as I waited for the message
count. I'd silently be praying, "Please, let it be good, let it be a
good one." Sometimes they were good – a parent wanting to share
how enthusiastic their son was about our newest unit. Other times
it was simply a field trip confirmation. But, every now and again,
the messages I received were bad ones. One time, a parent who
was very upset with the version of a playground incident their
child had related after school, demanded an explanation, despite
the fact that it was Wednesday and my supervision day was
Tuesday. Other complaints may have been a swear-word heard on
the field, a snide comment in the hallway over an outfit, or a
frustration with the Spring break calendar.

In my first year of teaching, I took each one of these calls as if they
were my own personal fault. If I were a better homeroom teacher,
my thirty-plus students wouldn't get into trouble on the
playground. If I were teaching enough character education,
swearing and teasing could never be attributed to my students.
The list could go on and on.

With each complaint or issue that was raised, the burden on my back became heavier as I placed the blame fully on my own shoulders. Because I was continually repeating this cycle, the phone became the most dreaded item in my classroom – even more dreaded than the sticky, smelly juice box recycling bin.

> I received each parent phone call as an attack.

What stopped this dangerous fear and self-burdening came through a lesson on Greek Mythology. No, it wasn't that Zeus or Aphrodite lived out some great wisdom that changed my life, but a scenario that occurred in the hallway five minutes before the much anticipated "Greek Fair" in my grade six classroom.

A particular mother greeted me in the hallway and proceeded to ask me, very pointedly, if I was countering all this teaching of Greek Gods and Goddesses with truth, or if I was teaching them as a valid and recommended belief system.

So many things about that encounter nearly brought me to tears – right there in the hallway between the staffroom and my classroom. The manner in which I was approached and questioned caught me off guard, to say the least. The fact that this mother would believe that I could honestly be capable of such biased instruction was insulting. Furthermore, she'd caught me at the beginning of a very exciting and stressful day, just before class was to begin, and it threw me for a loop – big time!

What really turned that incident around for me were the kind words of my teaching mentor. She imparted me some wise words that day that have served me well in my teaching.

Firstly, you need to consider the ratios. That one negative comment may be the only one from all 30 or so families represented in my classroom. That year, I had 26 students; therefore that ratio would have been 4%. Conversely, 96% is a pretty high

> Consider the ratios.

approval rating! I could even add a few more disgruntled parents. Even with five dissatisfied parents, 81% is the final ratio of satisfaction and I could still feel pretty good about my teaching.

The problem is, we never sit down and crunch the numbers. Furthermore, we never consider these topics in relation to ratios. Instead, we allow the squeaky wheel to get all the attention, and we adjust our practice, our activities, our teaching styles. Quite often, we allow our job satisfaction to suffer, all because of a small fraction of our total stakeholders.

The problem is that you don't hear from everyone all of the time. There are multiple and varied stakeholders that have an invested interest in the quality of education you are giving: students, parents, administration, etc. To base your feelings of success on solely one group of those stakeholders, or what is even more precarious, a single member of that grouping, typically only results· in feeling stressed, unappreciated and misunderstood.

> *You will never be able to please everyone.*

You will never be able to appease everyone, all of the time. Because of that, you need to keep proper ratios in mind when dealing with negative feedback. As my mom would say, "Consider the source; learn from it, and move on."

There is a wonderful children's book that paints this message beautifully. It is entitled "You Are Special", by Max Lucado. It talks about a people called the Wemmicks, who go around giving each other stars and dots all day long for their successes and failures. One particularly damaged and fraught Wemmick is especially susceptible to the judgements given by his peers. He reaches the conclusion that he must not be a very good wooden person because he simply cannot get stars from the others. He encounters a Wemmick with not a single sticker on her and learns that she spends time with the Carpenter who created all the Wemmicks with love. She's decided that what He thinks is more important than what the little Wemmicks think, and so, the stickers don't stick to her because they don't matter to her. "The stickers only stick if you let them," says the loving Carpenter.

Just as this is a great allegory for students, it was also a meaningful story for me as a teacher and as a human being. The stickers given to me by others only stick if I let them. A parent's complaint, a student's disdain for class, a former teacher's impossible example to follow, all those are stickers that will stick to me only if I let them.

> *The stickers only stick if you let them. Labels only define me to the degree I let them stick.*

Secondly, I learned that I can't be all things to all people, and the sooner I realized that the better. Each student I teach has a different personality, dozens of likes, dislikes and learning preferences. These are multiplied when you consider the personalities, likes, dislikes and learning preferences of their parents. I simply cannot excel in everyone's opinions and I most certainly should not try.

> *I can't be all things to all people, nor should I try.*

Another aspect to that is that I once believed that all these outside evaluators of my performance were omniscient. They should know the hours I spent on a project, or the reasoning behind a decision, or my heart's intention for responding to a problem in a certain way. Naturally, I could not expect them to know that information, and yet I was placing my career, my belief in my suitability as a teacher in their hands!

> *Outside evaluators are not omniscient; they do not see all the hidden factors that go into all your decisions, plans and actions.*

> *To give someone with such limited understanding power in determining our sense of success and satisfaction in our jobs is reckless and foolish.*

98

When we place our success in the hands of others, and also place unhealthy, unbalanced value on that judgement, it is actually a recipe for disaster in any profession. Rather than running on that never-ending treadmill of seeking approval, I had to learn to hold my job, my students, my evaluations and successes with open hands.

It sounds ironical, doesn't it? Holding on with open hands – but that is exactly what I mean. I had to learn to do my very best, and then release it. Let go and watch it unfold. The closer I held on to things, the tighter I clung to them, the more I sought the approval of others as a measure of success and the more I felt completely unsuccessful. Hold on with open hands, do your best, give it your all, and then release it, because it really was your best work, at that given time. When something didn't work out so well, even if something bombed,

> *I had to learn to do my very best, and then release it.*

then I could take it back, rework it for next year or the next week, and learn from it. However, if I didn't release it, I became weighed down with opinions and evaluations – even the good ones – because I relied too closely on performance. My identity was found to be too grounded in what I did. In holding on with closed hands and tight fists, what I did and how I performed became who I was, instead of the other way around.

> *Without releasing it, my identity as a teacher was tied too closely to performance.*

"Who I am" should never be negotiated by performance, nor opinions of students, parents, colleagues, or anyone else for that matter. Many of us turn to the teaching profession because we long to make a difference. It's a good thing that many of us are so interwoven and impassioned by our profession that it can have enormous positive repercussions in our lives. But, if we don't hold on with open hands, it can damage us deeply and set us up for early retirement.

> *"Who I am" should never, ever be determined by someone else.*

The third thing my teaching mentor taught me that day was to make appointments. I do not need to drop everything for an encounter in the hallway, but can and should schedule appointments with parents who wish to discuss something with me. That way, I will be more prepared for the encounter and I am not deflated before the day even begins. If a situation like this arises in the hallway, or by phone, I will ask them what they wish to discuss, and then invite them to make the appointment. That way, I have an idea of what is going to be discussed and we can talk at a time where we won't be interrupted. I have learned a similar approach to email. Often, emails can be damaging to communication because tone is never apparent and words cannot be explained. I have a

> *Make appointments to discuss areas of concern; you can be prepared and better set for success.*

response prepared ahead of time for parents who email me; I can it send quickly so that they feel that their concern has been heard, and invite them to make an appointment so that we can discuss it further.

The last thing I learned through that encounter in the hallway was that parents are not the enemy! By giving parents the power to dictate how I felt I was doing in my job, I distanced myself from them, almost in fear, and created a great divide between home and school. Instead, I need to embrace a strong partnership between home and school. By working together, efforts can be doubled and impact can grow exponentially. By using different strategies towards one ultimate goal, we can inspire learning and curiosity within the student.

> *We are in partnership with parents... a good partnership needs good communication.*

Reflection Questions:

1. Do I have an unhealthy fear regarding contact from parents or administrators? Why or why not?

2. When given feedback or input into your teaching practice, activities or field trip selections, you have a choice of what to do with it. Think of a time when you received particular feedback; write down responses to the following steps:

    a. What is the feedback that was received?

    b. From who was it received?

    c. Did you receive it in a negative or positive way?

    d. The giver of feedback – did they have a complete view of the situation or was their insight limited?

    e. What is the truth that you can extract from this feedback?

    f. Does this warrant change or action? Why or why not?

g. What can you do or change in response to the feedback?

h. Why are you going to make that change? What justifies it?

i. Why are you not going to make any changes? What justifies that?

j. Do you need to make another colleague or administrator aware of this – the feedback, as well as the way in which you are dealing with it?

k. Write a concluding statement so that you can let go of the incident or feedback, especially if you've taken it personally or feel as though it was negative. How can you "close the book" on this one?

In conclusion...

3. What is your response when a parent wants to talk about a given issue in the hallway?

4. What is your response to emails that are received from parents who want to discuss an issue via email?

5. Who is a mentor teacher or administrator you can go to, to discuss feedback received, in a safe manner and receive guidance about how to deal with certain situations?

6. Like in the story of the Wemmicks, what are the "stickers" that I have let stick to me? (note, they might all be bad)

7. How can I work at making sure that I don't let the "stickers" stick to me?

- Welcome feedback. Remember that no one is perfect, and even though a parent's comment may seem mean or attacking, they are basically fighting for what they believe to be best for their child. There is usually honour in what they are trying to do, even if they are not choosing the best way of communicating it.

- Remember that you are not what others say of you. Feedback is just that – feedback. It is a response that can, at times, be limited or very knowledgeable, but it is just that – a response.

- Choose to filter feedback using the questions in the reflection section, and decide to close the book once you have dealt with the given feedback.

- Build a rubric-rich assessment plan. The more that you can justify your marks, the greater credibility you earn in the parents' eyes. Rather than an arbitrary marker that bestows marks based on personality, favouritism, or any other accusations, by giving rubrics with your assignments even before students get started, you are creating an environment where students are responsible for their own achievement.

  > *-One time a student's father was very upset with the idea that I had students write an autobiography and then proceeded to give them a grade. How dare I mark their personal stories – how could each and every student NOT achieve a 100%? After I produced the rubric and assignment specifications that were explained and handed out when the assignment was introduced, the debate was over. The father could see how I was scaffolding learning,*

how I was giving the students design specifications and grading them on their abilities to meet those specifications adequately.

- Keep samples of your students' work. Although it takes up space in filing cabinets, it makes parent-teacher interviews a breeze when you can evidence marks with the exact work in front of you. Pairing the work with the corresponding rubrics enables parents to see what was asked of students, and they can clearly see how their child achieved the mark he/she was given.

Other Resources:

- Marnie Beaudoin, Sandra Carl-Townsend **Conversations About Assessment** *A Parent's Guide*. Available to order at http://www.aac.ab.ca/ConversationsParent.html

This small, concise parent's guide aptly explains the difference in formative and summative assessment in a way that parents can understand. It also helps to illustrate the role they can play in assessment at school. Well worth the investment, this guide should be given to each parent in your school as you are making the shift from summative to more formative ways of assessing.

- Glenn W. Olsen and Mary Lou Fuller, *Home-School Relations: Working Successfully with Parents and Families,* ISBN: 978-0205498406

This book outlines strategies and underscores the importance of strong home and school relationships.

8. Making Learning Meaningful
To <u>Never</u> Ask Why?

"What are you doing with the non-renewable life minutes of your students?"

Dr. Leah Fowler
University of Lethbridge

That question has haunted me with each lesson I plan, each activity I create, and each class novel I determine we will read. As Dr. Fowler spoke those decisive words in class, I decided right then and there that I wanted to strive for a classroom where students never ask, "Why are we doing this?" No – instead, I wanted to build a classroom where assignments were motivating, in and of themselves, and where the end result was something more tangible than a percentage grade or a completion checkmark in the grade book.

But how? It is not always easy, nor something I always get right – but keeping that goal in mind has really shaped my teaching. We could have a test at the end of the unit – or – we could create a museum in a box that would be displayed at the local public library. Creating the museum in a box challenges students to evaluate their learning on a deeper level, and the public display offers them a motivation to do it and do it well. Tasks, such as the museum in a box, sometimes called "Performance Based Tasks" or "Critical Challenges", call on students to recall information in a pertinent and practical manner, working towards a purpose. It is an "authentic method of instruction and evaluation whereby students apply knowledge and skills through practical demonstrations or creative products that illustrate learning".[11]

---

[11] Luongo-Orlando, Katherine. Pg 7. Authentic Assessment. Pembrooke Publishers, 2003.

In her book, Authentic Assessment, Katherine Luongo-Orlando states that "performance tasks present learners with real-world challenges" and allow "students to demonstrate a richer level of understanding and application of process and learning skills in a broader context than traditional testing would allow".[12] In other words, you can eliminate or significantly diminish your classroom discipline issues, as well as harness your students' energy and excitement, by creating exciting and enticing assignments.

> *You can eliminate or significantly diminish discipline issues in class by having engaging, motivating assignments.*

"Differentiated instruction is about making space, making space for meeting the individual needs of students to become even more powerful readers, making space for varied ways of demonstrating learning and achievement, making space for students to build knowledge of the world through questions that engage their imagination, and making space for practitioners to continue their own learning to refine instruction so that each student has opportunities to learn and show achievement."[13]

> *Each student needs to have the opportunity to learn and show their achievement.*

> *Students should never ask "Why are we doing this?"*

---

[12] Luongo-Orlando. Katherine. Pg 7-8. Authentic Assessment. Pembrooke Publishers, 2003.

[13] *Sandip Wilson*. Differentiated Instruction: How are design, essential questions in learning, assessment, and instruction part of it? **New England Reading Association Journal**. Portland: 2009. Vol. 44, Iss. 2; pg. 68, 8 pgs

You can see that differentiated instruction, performance based tasks, and critical thinking are all synonymous with a methodology in which students never ask the question, "Why are we doing this?"

There are countless other titles and frameworks that could be outlined here, but I encourage you to keep it simple and straightforward, and make the tasks in your class interesting by keeping this acronym in mind: **E-A-S-Y:**

Engaging – make sure that the assignment, worksheet, or research project is engaging. Are the students going to be motivated to do the work? Is there an outside arena where they can present, publish or showcase their work to make it even more meaningful?

Assessment Rich – is your grading criteria clear? Do students know exactly what they are going to be graded on and how? (Making the rubric together as a class ensures they understand the assessment plan.)

Structured for Success – make sure that your steps are clearly outlined. Don't assume your students will automatically understand. Find ways to communicate instructions in various ways. Also, make sure that you break larger assignments into smaller chunks and set small goals within the larger deadline.

Your Own – add your own flavour to assignments you find in textbooks, teacher guides or other resources. Also, ensure that students are able to add their own personal signature to their assignments, allowing for choice and multiple intelligences to shine.

Some assignment presentation formats:

Newspaper

Magazine

Multimedia Presentations:
- slide show
- web site
- digital pictures

Commercial

Radio Broadcast

TV segment

Documentary

TV/Radio news program

Media tools:

comics/cartoons
- editorial
- comics/cartoons
- advertisement

Primary Documents:

-first hand accounts

-letters

-diary

-journal

-historical news clippings

Biography

Trivia game

Timeline

Reports (e.g., news, lab)

Research project

Essays

Photo essay

Instructions/Guidebooks

Brochures

Picture books

Myth

Legend

Fairy Tale

Folktale

Visual Displays:

-murals

-paintings

-posters

-drawings

-diagrams

-illustrations

-sketches

-print making

-bulletin boards

-exhibits

Oral   presentations
using visual aids

Investigations

Demonstrations

Experiments

Puppets

Play

Dramatization

Pantomime

Choral speaking

Improvisation

Role Play

Writing in role

Dance sequence

Ensemble

Musical Composition

Poem

Song/rap

Masks

Scroll

Artifacts

Sculpture

Carving

Maps

Short musical

Soundtrack

Storyboard

Computer-generated charts
and Graphic organizers
- list
-flowchart
-charts
-graphs
-spreadsheets
-database
-table
-census
-histogram
-stem and leaf plots
-Venn diagram

Panel discussions

Group discussions

Talk show

Debate

Films/video

Film strip

Photographs

Audio recording

Interview

Survey

Towers

Bridges

Structures

Models

3D figures

Information cube

Puzzle

Table directly reprinted from pg. 11, Authentic Assessment by
Katherine Luongo-Orlando, Pembrooke Publishers, 2003.
Permission granted for publication of this book
This page is NOT TO BE PHOTO COPIED.

The following example, which you might find helpful, shows how I structure final projects after reading a novel in Language Arts class. It was used at the conclusion of reading "The Hobbit".

The Hobbit – Final Project

Option #1: Picture It!
You need to draw two of your favourite scenes from the novel "The Hobbit". You need to write **one** paragraph for each picture, explaining the drawing and why it is your favourite scene in the book.

Option #2: Time Capsule
You will write a letter to someone in the year 2110 – one hundred years from now – and will try to convince them to read "The Hobbit", explaining why. Your letter must be at least four paragraphs long.

Option #3: The Perfect Gift
You have been chosen to give an appropriate gift to three main characters from "The Hobbit". Choose your three characters and draw a picture of the gift you would give each of them. Each drawing must also have a paragraph explaining why your gift would be appreciated by that character.

Option #4: Coming to a Theatre Near You!
"The Hobbit" is coming out on film and you have been asked to design the movie poster. You need to think of the images you will use, which actors will be the main characters, and write a short summary of the film to try to attract viewers.

Option #5: Postcards from the Journey
You need to pretend that you are Bilbo Baggins on the journey to the cave of Smaug. Along your journey you will stop three times and write a postcard to someone special in your life. Your postcard needs to have an illustration on the front and at least ten sentences on the back, explaining where you are along your journey. Be descriptive – have fun!

Reflection Questions:
    1. Are my students actively engaged in class?

    2. If a stranger walked into the room and asked my students why they were completing a given task, would they be able to give their reason?

3. In my classroom, what are some assignments or activities that I do that are not good use of the non-renewable life minutes of my students?

4. Considering my answer to question #3, what meaningful activities can I replace the list with and still accomplish my curricular outcomes?

.

5. What area am I going to focus on to make learning more meaningful in my classroom – it can be a subject, a unit, or a routine you want to introduce.

Action Steps: Letting the roots go deep

- Don't reinvent the wheel, but choose an area in which you feel your classroom teaching or assignments lack particular vitality; seek to bring meaning to it. Keep the E-A-S-Y acronym in mind.

- Network – share great assignments with others in your school or district. If you each create one fantastic assignment for a different unit in grade three Science, together you can cover a lot more ground than you could ever on your own.

- Ask a colleague to read your assignments – make sure that they can understand your instructions, your purpose and your assessment plan. Ask them for feedback.

- Get to know your students – their likes and dislikes. Assignments can be easily tweaked to tap into what truly excites your students. For example, if you know that a student is musical or highly interested in music, instead of having them complete a written essay, have them demonstrate their knowledge of plot and theme for a novel by creating a soundtrack, complete with written instructions of how each song depicts a given plot point. Conversely, if you have a student who loves computers, allow them to complete their project on power-point, or create a web-quest for the class to enjoy. By tapping into their likes and hobbies, you have instant motivation for them to complete their assignments and complete them well.

Other Resources:

- Katherine Luongo-Orlando, *Authentic Assessment: Designing Performance-Based Tasks*, ISBN-13: 978-1551381527

One of my required reading books for university, this book offers tremendous examples of creating meaningful tasks for your classroom.

- Carol Ann Tomlinson*, Differentiated Classroom: Responding to the Needs of All Learners* 978-0-87120-342-7

A differentiated classroom is one in which the teacher knows and believes that students are unique and learn and demonstrate their learning in different ways. Carol Ann Tomlinson explains what that can look like and why it is so important in our classrooms.

- Anne Davies, *Making Classroom Assessment Work* , 978-0-9783193-2-8.

This book offers ideas and examples for assessment for learning, in other words, formative assessment, while also acknowledging the need for summative assessment. Anne Davies is an expert in this field and this book is a must read to understand the focus and importance on "Assessment" in education today.

- Kathleen Gregory, Caren Cameron and Anne Davies, *Knowing What Counts Series* (3 Books),

These three books illustrate ways teachers can involve their students in assessment and evaluation. They are filled with fantastic examples, ready-to-use blackline masters, and really equip you to do assessment well while involving your students in the process. The series includes the following three titles:

- *Setting and Using Criteria*   978-0-9682160-1-9
- *Self-Assessment and Goal-Setting*   978-0-9682160-2-6
- *Conferencing and Reporting*   978-0-9682160-3-3

9. Celebrate
Marking Milestones with Celebration

Celebrate what you want to see more of.

Thomas J. Peters

Do not ask yourself what the world needs:
Ask yourself what makes you come alive.
And then go out and do that.
Because what the world needs
Is people who have come alive.

Harold Whitman

The highest reward for man's toil is not what he gets for it,
But what he becomes by it.

John Ruskin

Teachers often shy away from showcasing the work of their students or their own phenomenally created assignments. Sometimes they can merely withdraw from such a stage because they genuinely feel afraid that they will appear boastful or grandiose; they tend to keep their successes to themselves. Another reason for such extraction can be fear of criticism.

This kind of individualism hurts us, as well as our profession. Celebrate learning, whether it is of your students or of yourself. In a staff meeting, share the light-bulb moment of one of your students. Contribute to the bulletin board space around the school and showcase the triumphs of

> *Teach your students to value the accomplishments of others*

your class. Write something for the school newsletter; invite other

119

classes to your culture fair day, or science fair. In doing so, you are teaching your students to value the accomplishments of others. Students learn to be observers of success, learn to ask relevant questions and learn to give positive encouragement and affirmation.

There is a lot of curriculum to cover, and the demands of the job can seem overwhelming before the year has even begun. The hours seem too short, and the desire to impart teaching and skill-building activities as much as possible is a definite temptation. But I strongly encourage you to take time to seize the meaningful moments. Take some time on Martin Luther King Jr. day to seize the opportunity to have a discussion about the reason for the day, the meaning of his cause and the historical turning points he inspired. Today's generation needs to be taught these things; they need to be enlightened. In a day of information overload, sometimes MSN chats, YouTube videos, and Facebook walls occupy far too much space in the

> *Take time for the extras.*

minds of our students instead of the meaningful moments in world history. Take time for the extras, for "those who cannot remember the past are condemned to repeat it".[14]

It is a great privilege to be an educator. You have a captive audience and the potential to mould hearts, inspire minds, and build solid foundations for the future. Never shy away from this great undertaking – meet it head on and seek to do the privilege justice. I hope that this book has somehow equipped you in this worthy task and encouraged you to be more reflective, stronger in your purpose and affirmed enough to weather the ups and downs that will come.

As you journey through those ups and downs, I challenge you to C-E-L-E-B-R-A-T-E. Don't shy away from celebration – a triumph for an individual in the classroom, an entire class success, or a personal victory with a certain child. Celebrate! Celebrate each

---

[14] Santayana, George. The Life of Reason, Volume 1, 1905

day; celebrate each class, each accomplishment and even each failure. Remember, we are all works in progress: your students, their parents, your administrators, and you – works of art that are forever in progress. I wish you well along the journey – keep on keeping on. I will leave you with a great poem that I hope inspires you on your journey.

I Didn't Know

I didn't know that years of school and a college degree would be of little consolation when facing a room full of bright little eyes on the first day of school. I thought I was ready...

I didn't know that five minutes can seem like five hours when there is idle time and an eight hour school day far too short for a well-planned day of teaching.

I didn't know that teaching children was only a fraction of my job. No one tells you about the conferences and phone calls, faculty meetings, committees, paperwork and paperwork...

I didn't know that it took so long to cut out letters, draw and color pictures, laminate-all for those bulletin boards that were always "just there"...

I didn't know that I would become such a scavenger, and that teaching materials would feel like pure gold in my hands...

I didn't know that an administration and co-workers that support and help you could make such a difference...

I didn't know that there would be children that I loved and cared for and stayed up late worrying about, who, one day, would simply not show up. And that I would never see them again...

I didn't know that I can't always dry little tears and mend broken hearts. I thought I could always make a difference...

I didn't know that the sound of children's laughter could drown out the sound of all the world's sadness...

I didn't know that children could feel so profoundly.
A broken heart knows no age.

I didn't know that a single "yes ma'am" from a disrespectful child or a note in my desk that says "You're the best!" could make me feel like I'm on top of a mountain and forget the valleys I forged to get there...

I never knew that after one year of teaching I would feel so much wiser, more tired, sadder and happier, all at once. And that I would no longer call teaching my job, but my privilege.

The work can wait while you show the child the rainbow, but the rainbow won't wait while you do the work.

                                                            Patricia Clafford

Reflection Questions:
1. Do I make time for celebration in my classroom?

2. What can I celebrate today? This week? This month? How am I going to choose to celebrate? (Share with a friend, special dinner, special night out, night without marking, etc.)

3. How can I encourage my students to celebrate?

4. How attached am I to time restrictions and curricular demands? Do I make time for teaching historical events or seizing teachable moments as they occur in the classroom?

- Celebrate! Look for opportunities for your students to celebrate, for your staff, and for you personally.

- Look ahead at the calendar; research historical days, and be aware of ways in which you can mesh your curricular outcomes with both current events and historical events.

- Draw your students into current events; inspire in them a love of the news and being a global citizen. Try to bring newspapers, newscasts and stories into your classroom. Be conscious of the balance between accomplishing curricular goals and educating citizens of this world. Sometimes we can be so driven by the textbook or teacher's guide that we become isolated from what is happening around us.

- Seize teachable moments as they come – through discussing a current event, de-briefing an incident on the playground, or discussing what you saw while celebrating the learning of another class by attending their presentation.

- Always strive to be a learner yourself. Choose professional opportunities wisely – you don't want to be overwhelmed – but look to refine your own practice by learning new methods, new technologies and new resources.

- Be inspired – by others, by books, by educational quotes, by whatever it takes to keep the joy fresh.

I hope you have enjoyed reading
"Beyond Survival: How to Thrive in Your First Years of Teaching"

I greatly value your feedback and would love to hear from you via email:
cheryl@gobeyondsurvival.com
or at Deep Roots Publishing
1-866-309-3622

Please let me know what has impacted you the most from reading this book, but also any areas that you still feel need to be addressed. I welcome your questions, comments and feedback.

Furthermore, I invite you to visit
www.gobeyondsurvival.com
for more publications from
Deep Roots Publishing.
There you will find study guides, classroom publications as well ongoing dialogue about current educational trends and issues.

Come and be a part of our own professional learning community!